The
Charles W. Morgan

The
Charles W. Morgan

THE WORLD'S LAST
WOODEN WHALESHIP

ANDREW W. GERMAN

ESSEX, CONNECTICUT

An imprint of Globe Pequot, the trade division of
The Rowman & Littlefield Publishing Group, Inc.
4501 Forbes Blvd., Ste. 200
Lanham, MD 20706
www.rowman.com

Distributed by NATIONAL BOOK NETWORK

British Library Cataloguing-in-Publication Information available

Library of Congress Cataloging-in-Publication Data
Names: German, Andrew W., 1950– author. | Mystic Seaport Museum.
Title: The Charles W. Morgan : the world's last wooden whaleship / Mystic
    Seaport Museum with Andrew German.
Other titles: World's last wooden whaleship
Description: Essex, Connecticut : Lyons Press, [2024] | Includes
    bibliographical references and index. | Summary: "As America's oldest
    merchant ship still afloat and the only wooden survivor of the
    once-vital whaling industry, Mystic Seaport Museum's flagship vessel,
    the *Charles W. Morgan*, tells a complex story-one that reflects our
    changing relationship with the natural world and with the diverse
    populations of the globe over two centuries of American history"—
    Provided by publisher.
Identifiers: LCCN 2023057607 (print) | LCCN 2023057608 (ebook) | ISBN
    9781493084432 (paperback) | ISBN 9781493084463 (epub)
Subjects: LCSH: Charles W. Morgan (Bark)—History. | Whaling ships—New
    England—History.
Classification: LCC VM465 .G47 2024 (print) | LCC VM465 (ebook) | DDC
    639.2/8092—dc23/eng/20240212
LC record available at https://lccn.loc.gov/2023057607
LC ebook record available at https://lccn.loc.gov/2023057608

Printed in India

Contents

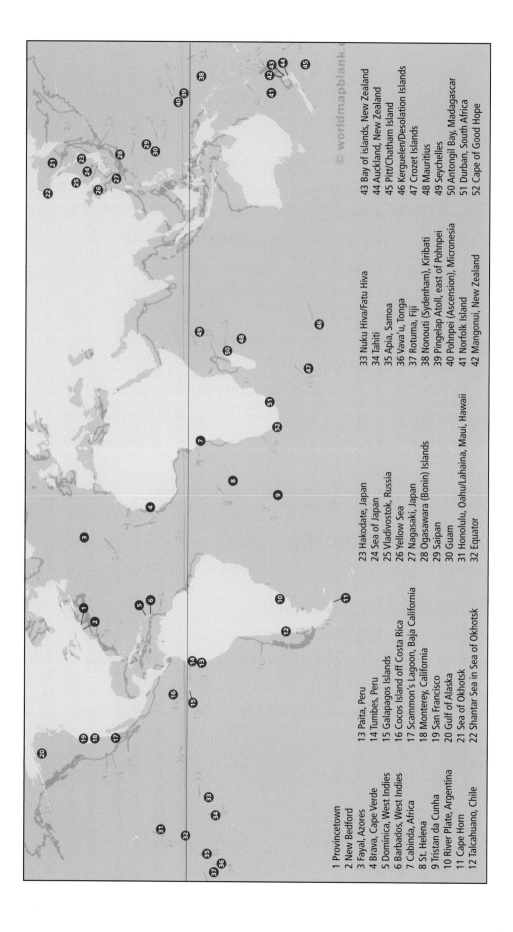

1 Provincetown
2 New Bedford
3 Fayal, Azores
4 Brava, Cape Verde
5 Dominica, West Indies
6 Barbados, West Indies
7 Cabinda, Africa
8 St. Helena
9 Tristan da Cunha
10 River Plate, Argentina
11 Cape Horn
12 Talcahuano, Chile

13 Paita, Peru
14 Tumbes, Peru
15 Galapagos Islands
16 Cocos Island off Costa Rica
17 Scammon's Lagoon, Baja California
18 Monterey, California
19 San Francisco
20 Gulf of Alaska
21 Sea of Okhotsk
22 Shantar Sea in Sea of Okhotsk

23 Hakodate, Japan
24 Sea of Japan
25 Vladivostok, Russia
26 Yellow Sea
27 Nagasaki, Japan
28 Ogasawara (Bonin) Islands
29 Saipan
30 Guam
31 Honolulu, Oahu/Lahaina, Maui, Hawaii
32 Equator

33 Nuku Hiva/Fatu Hiva
34 Tahiti
35 Apia, Samoa
36 Vava'u, Tonga
37 Rotuma, Fiji
38 Nonouti (Sydenham), Kiribati
39 Pingelap Atoll, east of Pohnpei
40 Pohnpei (Ascension), Micronesia
41 Norfolk Island
42 Mangonui, New Zealand

43 Bay of islands, New Zealand
44 Auckland, New Zealand
45 Pitt/Chatham Island
46 Kerguelen/Desolation Islands
47 Crozet Islands
48 Mauritius
49 Seychelles
50 Antongil Bay, Madagascar
51 Durban, South Africa
52 Cape of Good Hope

© worldmapblank.c

Foreword

Had it not survived against all odds, the New Bedford whaleship *Charles W. Morgan* might have faded into obscurity. Of the 750 whaleships that sailed out of New Bedford, 231 were lost: sunk, run aground, burnt, or simply disappeared. Others were abandoned or deteriorated until they were little more than a jumble of rotting planks. Most of the forty-five ships sent to blockade the Confederate ports of Charleston and Savannah in 1861 and 1862 as part of the first and second Stone Fleets were old and work-worn New Bedford whaleships sacrificed for the Northern war effort. But the *Charles W. Morgan* did survive, and this is its story.

Meticulously researched by Andrew W. German, this third book on Mystic Seaport Museum's flagship vessel expands on John F. Leavitt's foundational scholarship for the 1973 first book and the extensive revisions by German, with the assistance of Roger Hambidge and David Littlefield, for the 1998 second book. In this third account, German has expanded the narrative to include the perspectives of the women who sailed on nine of the *Morgan*'s thirty-seven whaling voyages, the diverse crews, the understanding of the whale as far more than prey, and the important role today of the world's single surviving nineteenth-century wooden whaleship. As the *Morgan* might say, in the words of the Biblical Job and in the epilogue to *Moby-Dick*, "And I only am escaped alone to tell thee."

The longest-serving member of the *Morgan*'s crew during its whaling years was boatsteerer John E. D. Smith, who joined the crew of the *Morgan* in 1868 and served on it for twenty-three years, missing only the 1887–1888 and 1888–1889 voyages before retiring in 1891. Smith put in more time and more miles aboard the *Morgan* than did any other individual. But, thanks to the remarkable series of circumstances that led to the preservation of the *Morgan* at Mystic Seaport Museum, I have spent on the *Morgan* double Smith's time (although not his miles). I have worked on the *Morgan* for forty-seven years as part of the demonstration crew, setting and furling sails high above the ship's deck and lowering and raising whaleboats from the ship's davits. I have spent more time aloft on this ship than any person, alive or dead. To quote *Moby-Dick* once more, "A whale-ship was my Yale College and my Harvard" (chapter 24).

I am lucky in that the visceral understanding of the work of a whaleship has not eluded me. Yet I have never sailed around Cape Horn. I have worked aloft in bitter cold and snow, but I have always had a refuge of warmth to retreat to afterward; I have not been forced to shiver with cold in a damp and desolate forecastle. The officers under whom I have worked have rarely acted like tyrants—and, if they had, I had the option of leaving. I accept, then, that my knowledge, although visceral, is limited.

Herman Melville, too, had a visceral understanding of the work of a whaleship. He knew not only whaling in the ways that have been extensively explored by scholars—aesthetically, morally, existentially—but also whaling kinesthetically. He spent four years at sea and served on three different whaleships. He knew what whaling was like with his feet and his arms and his hands. Enabling that visceral understanding is one of the many roles that the *Morgan* now serves at the Museum today.

The *Morgan* was built only seven months after and seven miles away from Melville's first whaleship, the *Acushnet*. The *Pequod* in Melville's 1851 masterpiece *Moby-Dick* is a fantastical ship, with its belaying pins made from sperm-whale teeth and a tiller fashioned from the lower jaw of a sperm whale: "a cannibal of a craft, tricking herself forth in the chased bones of her enemies," as Melville writes in chapter 16. Yet the very physicality of the *Morgan* gives us at least a faint understanding of what Melville encountered.

The *Charles W. Morgan* is important for many reasons. The resonance that the ship has with *Moby-Dick* is certainly one. Melville scholars and enthusiasts make the pilgrimage from around the globe to see the ship. The *Morgan* also represents a vital American industry, one that made New Bedford the wealthiest community, per capita, in the United States in the middle of the nineteenth century. Whaleships in search of whales went around the world, at times becoming the first to enter seas or land on islands never before encountered by Europeans. The crews of American whaleships were diverse, as documented in the crew lists included in this edition and explicated in the text. African Americans, West Indians, Pacific Islanders, Native Americans, Cabo Verdeans, and Azoreans served as boatsteerers (harpooneers), officers, and captains. Without the help of the indigenous people in the many ports and islands that the *Morgan* visited, whalemen would have died of thirst and hunger.

The *Morgan* no longer kills whales—and has not for over a century. Its last whaling voyage occurred in 1921. The ship now serves as a link to the whales, the people, the cultures, and the world encountered by whalemen. The *Morgan* was a thoroughly typical whaleship, for which I have always been grateful, since by its very unexceptional qualities we can learn so much about whaleships in general. It was built in New Bedford, the premier whaling port, in 1841, just before the peak of American whaling in 1846, when there were 730 active ships in the American whaling fleet. That very ordinariness helps us to better understand what the whaling industry was like for all those who intersected with it—aboard, ashore, or in the sea.

Mary K. Bercaw Edwards
Professor of English and Director of Maritime Studies
University of Connecticut
October 16, 2023

Acknowledgments

This history of the *Charles W. Morgan* was largely derived from logbooks and manuscript material in the G. W. Blunt White Library at Mystic Seaport Museum.

Photographs and information on various captains were provided by Miss Gertrude Landers of Chagrin Falls, Ohio, a granddaughter of Captain Thomas Landers, Mr. and Mrs. Neal Landers of Manchester, Connecticut, and Mrs. Marian Church of Rochester, Massachusetts. A portrait of Captain James A. Hamilton was given by James A. H. Campbell, while James A. Hamilton gave further material. Information on Captain and Mrs. James A. M. Earle was supplied by James W. "Jamie" Earle, their son, who sailed on one of the whaling voyages from the West Coast. Mrs. Norman Earle, whose husband was a younger son of the Earles, also contributed some reminiscences. Inez Shakman of Ventura, California, offered information on her ancestor, Henry Dally, a crew member on the *Morgan*'s first voyage. Charles F. Sayle, of Nantucket, provided several interesting photographs.

We are in debt to the New Bedford Whaling Museum, the Martha's Vineyard Museum, the San Francisco National Maritime Museum, and the New Bedford Free Public Library.

All photographs are credited to the museum or organization from which we secured them. In many cases, however, we have used photographs already in our files, obtained many years ago from different sources for which no record exists of the donor. Others, such as those originally made by Whaling Enshrined, were acquired by this museum prior to or at the time when negotiations were underway to bring the vessel to Mystic. Many of them are now owned by the New Bedford Whaling Museum. We are only too glad to acknowledge our debt to the various organizations and people mentioned above and to any others whose names may have inadvertently been omitted.

Innumerable Mystic Seaport Museum staff members have provided restoration, research, and interpretation work on the *Morgan* since 1941. This book stands in tribute to their efforts in the vessel's ongoing story. Museum photographers Dennis A. Murphy and Andy Price documented the *Morgan*'s restoration and thirty-eighth voyage, and their images are featured in this volume. Other Museum staff members who contributed essential editorial and logistical support include Mary K. Bercaw Edwards, Akeia de Barros Gomes, Paul O'Pecko, Mary Anne Stets, and Claudia Triggs. Brittany Stoner of Globe Pequot Press navigated the project from concept to completion.

A humpback whale sounds near the *Charles W. Morgan*, Stellwagen Bank, July 2014. PHOTO BY ANDY PRICE. (MYSTIC SEAPORT MUSEUM, D2014-07-0232)

CHAPTER 1

Chasing the Whale

It was 1840, and Charles W. Morgan wanted a new ship for his fleet. As he walked from his elegant new house, down through New Bedford's neat grid of streets on the way to his counting rooms on the waterfront, he could look around at one of the most prosperous cities in the United States. At the wharves and at anchor in the harbor lay the source of his and the port's prosperity: whaleships.

The ship that he would build—now the only survivor of its kind—was a typical whale-hunting and factory ship of the time. After thirty-seven voyages over eighty years, navigating most of the world's oceans and a sea of changes in the industry while gaining a reputation as a "lucky ship," the vessel would avoid the usual destruction due to obsolescence and become a monument to its former industry. For more than fifty years as a museum ship, it would emphasize the bravery and ingenuity of those who served on board (and the captains' wives who accompanied them). Then, with the recognition that industrial hunting threatened the whales themselves with extinction, Morgan's vessel would become a link to the grand mammals of the sea that were still largely a mystery to us. The vessel's role as a vehicle of human diversity also became clearer in light of all the ports at which it called and all the cultural contributions to New England that arrived by sea. Finally, after nearly ninety years as a stationary museum object, the vessel would make a thirty-eighth voyage, teaching a new generation how adept it was under sail and, in a greatly moving encounter with whales off the coast of Massachusetts, paying tribute to the creatures that had been its purpose for existence.

With the vastness of the oceans covering more than seventy percent of the earth's surface, some life forms evolved from sea to land and others from land to sea. Cetaceans—whales—originated from air-breathing land mammals with an even number of toes—which today include, bison, camels, pigs, and the whale's closest relative, the hippopotamus—and evolved into sea creatures over about ten million years, beginning about fifty-five million years ago. Some twenty-five million years ago, one group of cetaceans known as Mysticeti gradually shed its teeth and developed long, overlapping strips of baleen—composed of keratin, like that of human fingernails—on its upper jaw. While another group, the Odontociti, retained their teeth and consumed fish, squid, and other sea creatures, the Mysticeti lived off tiny crustaceans called copepods and krill, forcing water through the curtain of baleen to filter out mouthfuls of copepods. As they evolved further, whales developed thick coats of blubber, a specialized form of fat that insulates their bodies from the cold, provides buoyancy, and stores energy. They also developed wonderfully efficient lungs and circulatory systems, permitting some species to dive up to a mile deep and hold their breath for an hour or more. Long-lived, highly intelligent, and social, whales roamed all the seas and faced few predators for most of their existence.

Humans have been creatures of the sea for only a few thousand years. To them, the whale was a monster of unimaginable power, the creature that swallowed Jonah, and the embodiment of evil chaos. Ketos, or Cetus, to the Greeks, the whale later was dubbed leviathan for the ultimate sea serpent of mythology. Humans likely first encountered whales when corpses washed ashore.

Evidence is sketchy, but Inuits of the Eastern and Western Arctic may have been the first to hunt whales. In Europe, the Norse seem to have initiated the hunt, beginning sometime in the 800s, as they took to the sea as what we call Vikings. Their double-ended longships, either rowed or sailed, were well suited for the open sea, and smaller versions were fast and maneuverable for hunting whales along-shore. By the 1300s, the Basques on the shore of the Bay of Biscay had developed a whale fishery, apparently using boats derived from the Norse boats. By the early 1500s, Basque whalers were carrying their whaleboats aboard larger ships to hunt whales off Iceland and Greenland. As the English, Dutch, and the inhabitants of other northern European states began competing and seeking resources on the open sea, they adopted the Basque whaling techniques and developed their own whaling fleets, which were operating off Greenland and in the far north Atlantic off Spitsbergen in the Svalbard islands by 1600.

The aim of their voyages was obtaining the thick, oil-rich blubber of the right whale, Eubalaena, the largest of the baleen whales. The name may reflect the early belief that this was the "true" whale, although some speculate that the name right whale was given because they floated after they were killed and therefore were the "right" ones to hunt. There are three species of right whales: one found in the North Atlantic Ocean, one in the North Pacific, and one in the oceans south of the equator. With their bulbous bodies and thick blubber, right whales can grow to more than 140,000 pounds in weight and 50 feet in length during their natural lifespan of perhaps 70 years. The North Atlantic and North Pacific whales generally migrate north along the continental shelves in spring, returning south in the fall. Females breed every three to five years, during the winter, and give birth after a year. While these whales follow the same patterns and often gather closely together, they do not seem to have strong family bonds or social structure.

Using the techniques of the Basques, and possibly the Norse, hunters would approach a whale in their whaleboat and drive a harpoon into its body to attach a long line (rope) to the whale. Once the whale had exhausted itself in towing the boat around while trying to escape, the whalemen pulled themselves up to the whale and drove a long-shanked, sharp-bladed lance into the whale's heart or lungs, fatally wounding it. Brought alongside the whaleship, the dead whale's blubber would be stripped off, cut up, and packed in barrels. After a season of

As depicted on these painted tiles, Dutch whalers began to hunt right and bowhead whales off the coast of Spitsbergen (Svalbard) and then Greenland around 1600. The techniques of early Basque, Dutch, and English whalers, including the use of harpoons and lances wielded from six-man whaleboats, were later adopted by New England whalers. (MYSTIC SEAPORT MUSEUM, 1953.3080)

whaling, the ship would return to port, where the blubber was rendered—"boiled" in a pot—to separate the oil from the connective tissue. Although some of it might be used to make soap, most of the whale oil was sold to burn in lamps for illumination. The long fronds of flexible baleen might be saved for use in jewelry and decorative items. The rest of the whale—its muscles, organs, and bones—was abandoned to the sharks.

This industry was brought to North America by the English and Dutch colonists in the 1600s. With limited agricultural potential, New England became a base for those who harvested the sea for fish and whales. Already, the Native peoples of what was later settled as New England had moved from salvaging dead whales on the beach to chasing them alongshore in dugout canoes. Natives with whaling experience would be incorporated in the expanding New England whaling industry.

In the mid-1600s, during England's religious struggles, George Fox concluded that both the Church of England and the Puritans were wrong and that individuals could have direct spiritual contact with their God, without the intercession of a minister. In its opposition to war and its emphasis on the family and the increased role of women, the Society of Friends grew as a sect despite government opposition and derision for its "Quakers," who trembled before the Lord. Quaker communities and Quaker meetings—the group services without a leader, where anyone might be inspired to speak—came to New England in the 1660s and to Pennsylvania in the 1680s.

In 1659, a group of Massachusetts Quakers purchased the island of Nantucket and settled it as a Quaker enclave. Beginning as farmers and sheep-raisers, the settlers soon turned to the sea, gathering their settlement around the island's sheltered harbor. They seem first to have preyed on Atlantic gray whales that swam close to shore, with boats largely crewed by Wampanoag men. Within a few decades the gray whales were depleted. By 1700, in Nantucket—located 30 miles off the Massachusetts coast and near Nantucket Shoals, where right whales fed— residents had shifted to hunting right whales offshore, making short voyages in small, single-masted sloops.

According to early histories of whaling, a Captain Hussey was seeking right whales when his vessel was blown further out to sea, perhaps near the Gulf Stream. There his crew sighted and killed a species of whale they had not seen before. By taking the first sperm whale, they would change the industry.

Only a few dead sperm whales had washed ashore in Europe before 1700, so the species was largely a mystery. Now we know the present form of the sperm whale may have originated in today's Pacific Ocean about one hundred thousand years ago. It is likely that about two million sperm whales roamed the oceans before men began to hunt them. They are remarkably evolved creatures. The sperm whale has the largest brain of any species, living or extinct, and produces the loudest sound made by any creature. The whale's body withstands the intense pressure of its regular dives to more than a mile deep, and it can hold its breath for more than an hour during these dives.

The whale's long, narrow, underslung jaw has about forty conical teeth that fit into sockets on the upper jaw and are apparently used in catching the deep-swimming giant squid on which sperm whales feed. The sperm whale's long forehead and blunt "brow" cover a chamber that whalemen called the case and scientists call the melon, which is filled with waxy "spermaceti." Early investigators guessed the material was meant for reproduction, which led to the whale's popular name. It is now known the case assists in the whale's echolocation. The sperm whale breathes through one external nostril on the upper left surface of its forehead, and when it exhales the spray is blown diagonally forward, which helped whalemen identify sperm whales on the surface. The right, internal nasal channel has a set of "lips" that constrict to produce extremely loud clicks that travel for miles through the water column and are used for both echolocation and for communication. The sperm whale's eyes are set low and behind the jaw, leading some to suspect the whales may swim upside down in the depths to see the silhouettes of giant squid swimming above them. When they sleep, they usually rest vertically, tail down, just below the surface. When the whales surface from their dives, they defecate, incidentally delivering nutrients to the top of the water column. If their digestive system is irritated by the sharp beaks of the squid they consume, they form a waxy material called ambergris, which would become highly valuable among humans for medicinal purposes in Asia and as a fixative for scent in perfumes in Europe and the Americas.

Sperm whales are social creatures, communicating widely through patterns of clicks and living in "pods" of between six and twenty individuals. The pods are made up of females and juveniles, and each pod has its own identifying pattern of clicks. When males mature at about age eighteen, they leave the pod to live on their own. These "bull" sperm whales tend to live in higher latitudes and find and engage with pods only when mating.

Except for the threat of killer whales (orcas) when they are young, sperm whales are free from natural predators and live for about seventy years. When a male reaches full size at around age fifty, he will be about fifty feet long and weigh roughly fifty tons (one hundred thousand pounds). A full-size female is about thirty-six feet long and weighs fifteen tons (thirty thousand pounds). Sperm whales eat about three percent of their weight each day, meaning three thousand pounds of squid for a large bull.

———◦◇◇◇◦———

As the search for sperm whales took them farther offshore, Nantucket whalemen in the 1750s developed the onboard furnace called a tryworks in which to render the oil from the blubber at sea. By then, they had determined how to process sperm-whale oil into extremely fine, bright-burning, smokeless lamp oil and the spermaceti into the best candles. These products were so valuable that sperm whaling spread to other New England ports. In 1765 it came to the settlement of Bedford on the Acushnet River in southeastern Massachusetts.

Joseph Rotch of Nantucket financed a candle works at Bedford that year and then relocated his whaling firm there in 1769. During the American Revolution, British forces burned Bedford during a raid. After the war, it was rebuilt and incorporated as New Bedford in 1787. In the 1780s, Joseph Rotch's grandson William Rotch Jr. took over the family operations there, and in the 1790s William Rotch Sr. and his son-in-law Samuel Rodman moved their large Nantucket whaling business there. Their Quaker families expanded, partly through marriage with prominent Quaker families from Philadelphia, and other non-Quaker merchants established whaling firms and their allied businesses in the growing Massachusetts port.

As the world's whaling industry had expanded in the 1700s, British and American whalers ventured south, discovering new whaling grounds off Brazil. After the American Revolution, the hunt resumed. In 1791, New England whalemen followed the British around Cape Horn and into the Pacific as well as around the Cape of Good Hope and into the Indian Ocean. By 1818, they had found the sperm-whale habitat along the equator in the Pacific, extending the hunt to the Sandwich

(Hawaiian) Islands in 1819, to Japanese waters in 1820, and to New Zealand and the Gulf of Alaska in the 1830s.

As the hunt for whales expanded, so did the demand for whale products. In 1812, the US Treasury Department had begun to purchase sperm-whale oil to light the nation's growing number of lighthouses—a number that increased from 55 in 1820 to 256 in 1842. After the War of 1812, with the growth of international and coastal trade, the market for whale products grew, and, with the opening of the Erie Canal and, eventually, the railroad, the whole Midwest had access to such coastal products. New England's growing textile industry, and the growth of American manufacturing overall, created a demand for very fine lubricants, with sperm oil becoming the oil of choice.

By the early 1820s, New Bedford's whaling fleet was larger than Nantucket's and would continue to grow. The community grew as well, with a grid pattern rising up the ridge from the waterfront to County Street on top of the ridge. In 1836, it received an imposing new granite customhouse, and the railroad reached New Bedford in 1840. The waterfront was lined with sixteen wharves, most of which were devoted to whaling. By 1841, New Bedford had twenty-one candle works and whale-oil factories. Its whaling fleet made it the fourth-largest port in the United States, after New York, Boston, and New Orleans. By 1839 the population was 12,354, and New Bedford was considered the wealthiest community, per capita, in the country.

Under the influence of the Quaker faith, New Bedford became a refuge for fugitives from slavery in the South. In 1839, 1,051 African Americans lived there, and others continued to arrive surreptitiously, aided by abolitionists in the community. In 1838, a Black man named Frederick Bailey, who had become skilled as a ship caulker in Baltimore, escaped enslavement and rode the train north, disguised as a sailor. Sent on to the abolitionist stronghold of New Bedford, he recalled visiting the wharves:

> I found myself surrounded with the strongest proofs of wealth. Lying at the wharves, and riding in the stream, I saw many ships of the finest model, in the best order, and of the largest size. Upon the right and left, I was walled in by granite warehouses of the widest dimensions, stowed to their utmost capacity with the necessaries and comforts of life. Added to this, almost everybody seemed to be at work, but noiselessly so, compared with what I had been accustomed to in Baltimore. There were no loud songs heard from those engaged in loading and unloading ships. I heard no deep oaths or horrid curses on the laborer. I saw no whipping of men; but all seemed to go smoothly on.

He continued, "From the wharves I strolled around and over the town, gazing with wonder and admiration at the splendid churches, beautiful dwellings, and finely-cultivated gardens; evincing an amount of wealth, comfort, taste, and

A portion of the New Bedford waterfront, as depicted in the "Grand Panorama of a Whaling Voyage 'Round the World," painted by Benjamin Russell and Caleb Purrington, ca. 1848. At right is the tall spire of the Baptist Church, and at left a flag identifies the Seaman's Bethel on Johnny-cake Hill. Charles W. Morgan's grand house with cupola on County Street stands on the horizon at left-center. His counting rooms were on Rotch's Square, along the waterfront at right. Whaleships fill the harbor. (IMAGE COURTESY OF THE NEW BEDFORD WHALING MUSEUM)

refinement, such as I had never seen in any part of slaveholding Maryland." He even found many of the city's recently arrived fugitives from slavery "living in finer houses, and evidently enjoying more of the comforts of life, than the average of slaveholders in Maryland."

Herman Melville, who came to New Bedford in the winter of 1840 to go to sea, agreed. "The town itself is perhaps the dearest place to live in, in all New England. It is a land of oil, true enough," he suggested in his whaling novel, *Moby-Dick*. "Yes, all these brave houses and flowery gardens came from the Atlantic, Pacific, and Indian oceans. One and all, they were harpooned and dragged up hither from the bottom of the sea." Melville was especially taken by the Seamen's Bethel, built in 1832 as a nondenominational church for seamen. Its walls were covered with ceno-taphs commemorating whalemen who had died at sea.

But, as a seaport with a large, transient population of sailors between voyages, New Bedford had another side, which is suggested in Melville's reference to the "har-pooneers, cannibals, and bumpkins" one might encounter in the street. Melville's Spouter-Inn represents one of the numerous boardinghouses that catered to sailors, often run by widows or African Americans. But he did not mention the more than fifty "grog" shops, in which sailors might find alcohol, or a similar number of houses of prostitution. From their fine homes on the hill, whaling merchants dealt with this side of their community through the temperance society and the Port Society for the Moral Improvement of Seamen, and even Charles W. Morgan occasionally paid the boardinghouse bills for his crewmen.

——◇◇◇◇◇——

Born into a Quaker family in Philadelphia in 1796, Charles Waln Morgan had married his sister-in-law Sarah Rodman and moved to New Bedford in 1819. Sarah Rodman Morgan was the daughter of whaling merchant Samuel Rodman and granddaughter of William Rotch, the leading Nantucket and then New Bedford whaling merchant. With this connection to the heart of New Bedford's whaling industry, Charles Morgan began his whaling investments in 1820, and by 1840 he managed nine vessels, making him the second-leading manager of whaleships in the port. Morgan also operated one of the port's candle-making enterprises and whale-oil processing plants. Morgan supplied sperm oil to the US Lighthouse Establishment through the 1830s. He tried to expand his profits from whaling through investments in Massachusetts and Pennsylvania textile mills, a paper mill, ironworks, coal mines, railroads, banks, and insurance companies. He also purchased land in the Midwest. In New Bedford, he was a director of two banks and frequently made private loans, especially to New Bedford's Black businesspeople.

Although he left the Quaker faith to become a Unitarian, he remained a trustee of Friends' Academy. His commitment to the community was expressed through his support for the New Bedford Free Public Library, the Lyceum, the temperance society, and the Port Society for the Moral Improvement of Seamen. While he spent much of his time managing business at his counting rooms on Rotch's Square along the waterfront, he could return at day's end to one of New Bedford's finest houses and gardens uphill along County Street, where the principal merchants

Charles Waln Morgan (1796–1861) as a young man, by an unidentified artist. (MYSTIC SEAPORT MUSEUM, 2004.48.1)

built their homes. Morgan had time for walks, reading literature, and contemplating the moral issues of the day, including the abolition of slavery—"what a curse this slavery has been to the *whole* country" he would write in 1850. Yet, like most New Englanders, he did not recognize the connection between his investment in and profits from cotton mills and the Southern slavery that produced the cotton for those mills.

When the fugitive Frederick Bailey was reunited with his wife at New Bedford, he resided with the free Black couple Nathan and Mary Johnson, who had worked as domestic servants for Charles W. Morgan before opening a business, and who lived a few blocks away from Morgan. Johnson encouraged Frederick to take the surname Douglass, and as Frederick Douglass he sought work as a caulker. Despite New Bedford's reputation as a haven for free Blacks and fugitives from bondage, Douglass found that the port's caulkers would not accept a skilled Black man. With Johnson's encouragement, Douglass would become a skilled orator and compelling advocate for the abolition of slavery. By 1840, he was listed as a minister in the city directory. Until he embarked on his new career as a principal spokesman for the abolition of slavery in August 1841, he and his family lived near the shipyard operated by Jethro and Zachariah Hillman.

CHAPTER 2

Building a Ship
1840-1841

In the fall of 1840, America was still in the middle of an economic depression resulting from the Panic of 1837. The United States of America was just a fraction of what it would become, with a population a bit over seventeen million. With twenty-six states in the Union, Arkansas and Missouri were on the edge of the western frontier. Florida was a territory, Texas was an independent republic, and California was a state of Mexico. William Henry Harrison was about to defeat Martin Van Buren for the presidency. Cotton was the nation's most important commodity, produced in the slavery-based agricultural economy of the Southern states.

Despite the weak economy, in 1839 the price of sperm-whale oil reached its highest point since the War of 1812, and the demand for "whalebone" (baleen) had increased five hundred percent since 1834. New Bedford already had about 150 ships, thirty-nine barks, and eight brigs in its whaling fleet, but the leading whaling agents like Charles W. Morgan were eager to expand their business.

The Hillman Brothers had opened their shipyard at the foot of Maxfield Street, above the bridge to Fairhaven, in 1826. Specializing in whaling vessels, they completed about one a year. By 1852 they would construct seventeen. It is likely that Morgan and the Hillmans discussed the dimensions and characteristics of the vessel Morgan desired. He wanted a fast, stable vessel with a large capacity for whale oil, so the hull would have a relatively flat bottom and "hard turn of the bilge." While broad above the waterline for buoyancy, the bow was narrow below and tapered smoothly back as the hull widened. Toward the stern, a long "run" narrowed the hull smoothly back to the rudder, making a hull that would move well through the water while carrying a lot of cargo. The hull below the waterline would be covered with thin copper sheets, an expensive addition intended to protect the hull from boring worms and marine growths. To protect the vessel from rot, salt would be packed into the spaces between frame timbers. With a length on deck of 105 feet and a beam (width) of 27 feet, the vessel would be typical in size for a whaleship.

To design the vessel for construction, the Hillmans likely carved a precise half-model from which all of the dimensions would be expanded to produce full-scale patterns on the mold loft floor of the shipyard. These patterns or molds were then used to shape the vessel's structural timbers, or frames (ribs).

The Hillmans probably laid the keel of Morgan's new vessel on the sloping ways of their yard at the end of December 1840. After the oak keel was laid, the oak frames

The view aft in the restored hold, looking as it did when the *Charles W. Morgan* was built in 1841. The stanchions at right show wear from the chafing of oil casks during whaling voyages.

PHOTO BY ANDY PRICE. (MYSTIC SEAPORT MUSEUM, D2-13-06-0621)

were set upon it and an interior keel, or keelson, was placed atop the bottom frame sections to sandwich them for strength. In this traditional form of construction, the frame sections overlapped each other, making a nearly solid skeleton. As the frames rose, the plankers shaped durable longleaf yellow pine from the South into bottom planks 3.75 inches thick and top planks 2.75 inches thick. The interior planking, or ceiling, added further strength to the hull. The quality of the ship was represented by Morgan's choice of expensive copper fastenings supplied by Anthony Richmond for the planks—two in each frame for a total cost of $3,240.98. Copper fastenings were not subject to the corrosion that would occur from using iron fastenings. Strong locust trunnels (tree nails) were also used as plank fastenings. To attach and support the beams for the vessel's two decks, right-angle knees cut from the root-trunk connection of the hackmatack (larch) tree were fastened at both sides and below the ends of each beam.

The workforce included the shipyard's core of ship carpenters skilled in the use of the adze and the broadax, some day laborers, and specialized tradesmen like joiners (finish carpenters), caulkers (who sealed all the seams between planks), sparmakers, and riggers, who worked by the job at various shipyards. At least thirty-one men contributed work as the vessel took shape. Samuel Damman, an

experienced shipwright, put in 177.25 days at a high daily rate of as much as $2.25 a day (when $2.00 a day [about $70.00 in 2023] was a skilled man's pay). Hervey Cables worked 173.5 days, for which he received $240, paid once or twice a month depending on his work. Mendall Ellis earned $258.33 for 144.5 days, Restcome Case worked 81.25 days for $155, and Patrick Boyles put in 287.25 days and took $5.50 of his $224 in the form of a barrel of flour. Black laborer James Scott worked for 133.75 days on the ship for $1.25 a day.

While their pay was standard in the field, the shipwrights had grievances. In April 1841, the port's shipwrights went on strike to further their demand for a ten-hour workday, an aim of the nation's new trade-union movement, at a time when the workday lasted from sunup to sundown, six days a week. Charles Morgan led the opposition to a shortened workday, but, after two weeks of negotiating, the two sides settled on a 10.5-hour day, and the men went back to work. With this delay, it took about seven months to build the vessel. In the end, Morgan spent $6,015.71 for labor on his ship, in addition to another $2,001.85 to the Hillman brothers for their labor and management, use of their yard, and some of the ship's timber.

In addition, caulkers James Drew, Isaiah Potter, Isaac Benjamin, George Clark, and George Wadsworth spent thirty-seven to forty-four days each, driving oakum (tarred hemp fibers) into all the seams between the planks and sealing them with pitch for a total of $424.50. Housewrights David Field and Lewis Hathaway did the finish carpentry in the living quarters throughout the ship for $588.02, and Thomas Tobey and William Maxfield painted the ship for $697.84. Despite the seafaring tradition of representing the vessel's name with a carved figurehead at the bow, Quaker practice called for unostentatious decoration so, like most whaleships, Morgan's ship was fitted with a simple billethead scroll carved by Henry Smith for about $18.00.

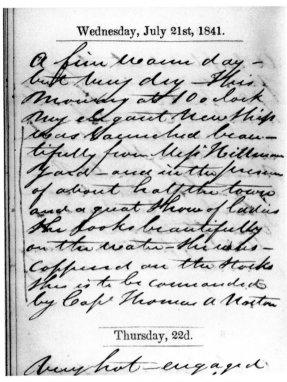

Charles W. Morgan recorded the launch of his new ship in his diary. (MYSTIC SEAPORT MUSEUM, 1966-5-42)

Whaleships were commonly owned by shareholders, and so was Morgan's new ship, with its value divided into sixteen shares. Charles W. Morgan took eight shares, or half the value, and acted as managing owner. Morgan's father-in-law, merchant Samuel W. Rodman, took two shares, as did the ship's planned captain, Thomas A. Norton. Morgan's nephew Samuel Griffitts Morgan and Samuel's business partner William G. E. Pope also took two shares, because they had supplied sailcloth, copper, iron, cordage, and oil casks and their hoops through their commission merchants' business. As the ship's builders, the Hillman brothers retained a sole share, and merchant and whale-oil gauger David Brayton took the remaining single share.

On July 21, 1841, Charles Morgan celebrated the vessel's launch in his diary: "This morning at 10 o'clock my elegant new ship was launched beautifully from Messr Hillman yard—and in the presence of about half the town and a great show of ladies. She looks beautifully on the water—she was coppered on the stocks." When it came time to rig the ship as a three-masted square-rigger, William Beetle shaped the masts and yards and set them up for $929.02. Joseph and Thomas Taber carved the many blocks (pulleys) for the lines that operated the sails for $730.66. Rigger Nathaniel Cannon set up both the heavy, tarred standing rigging that supported the masts and the running rigging that would operate the sails for $390.10. As a full-rigged ship, the vessel carried four square sails—from bottom up, the course, topsail, topgallant, and royal—on each of its three masts. For sailing to windward, and to assist in steering, as many as four triangular jibs could be set on the stays (standing rigging) between the bowsprit and foremast, with additional fore-and-aft sails on the stays between the masts. The mizzen (aftermost) mast also carried a fore-and-aft spanker set with a gaff and boom. To increase the area of the square sails for downwind speed, studding sails could be set from light booms outboard of the square sails. Sailmaker Charles Haffords stitched up and roped the edges of the sails by hand for $561.56.

Morgan paid Joseph Delano $1,202.67 for 14,900 pounds of anchor chain plus the fluke chain that would be used in whaling. Jacob Parker supplied the anchors and the two iron try-pots for rendering the whale oil for $737.30, and Gibbs Taber and Frederick Underwood set the try-pots into the brick tryworks they built on the ship's deck near the foremast. Morgan calculated the finished cost of his new ship as $26,877.78 (about $940,000.00 in 2023).

To outfit the ship for sea, Morgan purchased barrels of salt-preserved beef and salt pork, bushels of potatoes, bunches of onions, barrels of flour, gallons of molasses, and four hundred barrels of drinking water as well as an iron camboose (galley stove) for cooking. For navigating the vessel, he purchased maps, charts, compasses, a sextant for celestial navigation, an extremely accurate chronometer or ship's clock, and a copy of James Espys's new book on meteorology, *The Philosophy of Storms*. To maintain the crew's health at sea, he obtained a well-stocked medicine chest from Benjamin Coombs and William Wells for $75.04. Since the crew would need to purchase new clothes, tobacco, and other items at sea (for which they would be assessed interest until the items were paid off at the end of the voyage), Morgan purchased $570.41 worth of these "slops" from Joshua Richmond, Captain Thomas Norton, and the "ladies clothing store" operated by the women of the Port Society for the Moral Improvement of Seamen.

Since casks or barrels, large and small, would hold the ship's water and supplies, as well as the whale oil it would take, Morgan paid $3,281.03 to various suppliers for these oak containers. Many were fully coopered (set up), but the smaller oil casks might be purchased in the form of "shooks," or sets of staves and hoops that would be set up by the ship's cooper during the voyage. For whaling itself, Morgan purchased five cedar whaleboats for $467.24 and a supply of harpoons and lances from Howard Nichols for $185.00. He calculated the outfitting cost at $25,908.89. This makes the estimated total cost of the ship, when ready for sea, $52,786.67 (roughly $1,840,000.00 in 2023).

No name had been chosen for the new ship at the time of its launch, but, when Charles Morgan departed town as the ship was rigged and fitted out, Samuel Griffits Morgan gave it his uncle's name. "I don't altogether like it," remarked the unostentatious owner, but he did not change it.

CHAPTER 3

A Traditional Voyage and a Transitional One
1841–1848

merican whaling voyages were structured as joint ventures between each ship's owners and its crew. Each voyage was an adventure, as the length of the voyage, the catch, and its value in the marketplace could not be predicted; so, rather than working for a set wage, all shared in the risk and the reward. Generally, the owners or their agent provided the vessel and equipment and stocked it with basic seagoing provisions. The crew brought varying levels of expertise and were signed on for a share, or lay, representing the fraction of the value of the cargo they would receive at the end of the voyage.

As the most experienced man on board, and the one representing the owners' interests, the captain generally received a lay of about 1/15th, in addition to his portion of the stakeholders' shares. Depending on how many whaleboats the ship carried, there could be as many as four mates, who commanded the boats and killed the whales, for shares ranging from about 1/25th to 1/75th. Below them were the men generally called boatsteerers, who harpooned the whales for shares of about 1/95th.

Whaleships carried a carpenter to mend the vessel during its long voyage, a cooper to tend the wooden casks (barrels) in which the supplies were kept and the whale oil was stored, a cook to prepare three meals a day, a steward to serve the captain and mates, and sometimes a sailmaker to repair the sails and a blacksmith to repair the ironwork on board. Called idlers, as they did their daily work and were not part of the watches or boats' crews, their shares ranged between 1/55th and 1/125th. Most whaleships carried a few able-bodied seamen who knew how to steer a ship, were experienced aloft in setting, reefing (shortening), and furling the sails, and had a sailor's rope skills, with a lay of 1/120th. The crew also included ordinary seamen who had been to sea before but were not yet fully experienced and reliable, so they received about 1/150th. At the bottom were the "greenhands," who were making their first voyage and were largely ignorant of the ways of the sea. Until they gained experience, they were simply laborers, and their lay was about 1/180th. Added together, these lays would give the crew about thirty percent of the

In this detail from Benjamin Russell and Caleb Purrington's 1848 whaling panorama, a whale-ship flying Charles W. Morgan's house flag has studding sails set in the channel between Faial and Pico in the Azores. It could represent the *Charles W. Morgan*, though the *Morgan* is not known to have been painted with gunports as shown in the panorama. (IMAGE COURTESY OF THE NEW BEDFORD WHALING MUSEUM)

proceeds of the voyage, with the other seventy percent going to Morgan and the other owners.

Although the growth of the industry had changed the method of procuring labor from a community-based approach to a more universal approach that depended on wandering, largely unskilled, impressionable young men like Herman Melville to fill out crews, the *Charles W. Morgan*'s first crew fit the old model. Morgan already knew his choice as captain. Thirty-two-year-old Thomas A. Norton of Edgartown, Martha's Vineyard, had made his first voyage as captain in Morgan's ship *Hector* in 1834. A member of an old Martha's Vineyard family, Norton found at least four-teen island men to join the crew. One of them, fifteen-year-old Zenas Gould, of Wampanoag ancestry, represented the Native American roots in whaling. Second Mate James C. Osborn, thirty-six, whose journal details the voyage, brought along a library of more than seventy books, including memoirs, histories, travel books, James Fenimore Cooper's *Pathfinder*, and Captain Frederick Marryat's twenty-two

Captain Thomas A. Norton (1809–1885) brought a crew from his home island of Martha's Vineyard for the *Charles W. Morgan*'s first voyage. (COURTESY OF THE MARTHA'S VINEYARD MUSEUM)

books of fiction. First Mate Charles Chadwick, thirty-seven, was from Nantucket rather than Martha's Vineyard, and he had a solid background in whaling. Despite his New England name, George Morgan was a native of Tahiti who had arrived in New Bedford on an earlier whaling voyage.

In preparation for sea, crew members were usually supplied with a sea chest, a straw-filled "donkey's breakfast" mattress, and a basic outfit of clothing, tobacco, and necessities. These items were provided by the owner at a price that would be deducted from their pay at the end of the voyage, plus interest on the advance for the duration of the voyage. The "foremast hands" took their sea chests down the companionway into the forecastle (or fo'c'sle) bunk room at the bow. Lined with double-deck bunks, with the sea chests as seats in front, this would be the dark, sometimes wet home for the men for the duration of the voyage.

The officers moved into their quarters at the stern. The captain had a private stateroom with a water closet to starboard (right) and a furnished day cabin across the stern. The first mate had a private stateroom on the larboard (left) side, with a desk for keeping the ship's logbook. The second and third mates shared a stateroom forward of that. The staterooms opened onto the officers' mess room, with its table and benches, and the steward's pantry forward of it. Overhead, a large skylight provided plenty of light, unlike in the fo'c'sle. The skylight also housed a telltale compass so the officers could look up and see what course the ship was steering.

Forward of the mess room, several bunkrooms housed the boatsteerers and the idlers. As the galley (cookhouse) was probably in a small structure forward along the larboard rail at this time, the cook may have lived near it in the forecastle.

The *Charles W. Morgan* departed New Bedford on September 6, 1841, with all hands at work stowing provisions and gear and setting sail for the first time. They would find that the *Morgan* was a fast ship, and the vessel's logbooks record speeds of up to 9.5 knots (about thirteen miles per hour), which was good for a full-bodied ship with a one-hundred-foot waterline length.

The sea day began at noon, and at noon of that first day began a routine that would last, with little variation, for the ship's entire career at sea. First, the crew was divided into two watches under the first and second mates for operating the vessel during alternating four-hour work periods—watches—round the clock. During each watch, the passing of time (possibly measured by a half-hour sandglass) was marked by the ship's bell each half hour, from one bell to eight bells. At eight bells, the watches changed, and those with experience would take one-hour shifts at the wheel, while the rest learned the place of all the lines that operated the sails, handled the canvas sails themselves, and performed maintenance under their mate's supervision.

At the wheel, the helmsman would find that the ship had a very simple steering mechanism. The tiller, a horizontal lever attached to the head of the rudder, was attached to a tiller rope that ran through blocks. The ship's steering wheel was mounted on top of the tiller, with the tiller rope wrapped around an attached drum. Turning the wheel turned the drum and wound the tiller rope, moving the tiller and rudder. This simple, "shincracker" steering arrangement required the helmsman to sidle left or right as he stood beside the wheel, gripping the spokes. The helmsman usually kept his eyes on the compass mounted in the skylight in front of the wheel in order to steer a compass course as directed by the mate. Sometimes the helmsman was ordered to steer "full and by," in which case he kept his eyes on the sails to keep them full while steering as close as possible to the direction of the wind.

In either morning or afternoon, the crew "holystoned" the sacrificial planks nailed over the deck, washing and scrubbing them with large, coarse stones. Normally the whole crew was on duty from breakfast until the "dog watch," two two-hour watches beginning at 4 p.m. This was the crew's recreational and supper time, and it made for an odd number of watch periods, so the watches alternated the midnight-to-four duty. Off duty, the foremast hands had freedom of the deck forward of the mainmast; the after deck was the officers' area.

The officers had many daily navigation duties to track their course and position at sea. The mate, who kept the ship's logbook, made note of the compass course sailed.

In addition, he would have the sailors cast the logline, which had knots spaced to determine the ship's speed in knots, or nautical miles per hour, as it unreeled, timed by a fourteen- or twenty-eight-second sandglass. With course, speed, and time, the captain could track the vessel's course on a chart using dead reckoning.

To determine the ship's latitude, or distance north or south of the equator, the captain and first mate commonly "shot" the sun with their octants or sextants at local apparent noon, when the sun was at its highest point, or zenith, to find the sun's angle of elevation above the horizon. They used the difference between local apparent noon and the time on the ship's chronometer—a very accurate seagoing clock—to calculate their longitude, or distance east or west of the prime meridian.

At night, the captain and mate would again use their octants or sextants to measure the angles between the moon, stars, or planets and the horizon, then use the tables in a navigation book to determine a line of position. By triangulating several lines of position, they could establish the ship's position in relation to their dead reckoning. Repeating this process each day and relying on dead reckoning when they could not see the sun, moon, or stars, they navigated the *Morgan* across tens of thousands of miles in the open sea.

Within days of their departure, the sailors were divided into crews for the whaleboats and began to go aloft as lookouts to scan the horizon for the spouting of whales. The call "There she blows!" or "She blows!" from the lookout was the signal for the sailors to become whalemen. The ship carried four double-ended whaleboats, each about twenty-six feet long, hanging from pairs of davits along the rail: three on the larboard side and one aft on the starboard side. Each boat was lowered and raised with a pair of removable blocks and tackle, down which the crew climbed to man the boats. The ship also carried a couple of spare boats on a framework above the deck called the skids.

As they had evolved, whaleboats were awkward but efficient killer boats. Normally they were rowed with five long oars and steered with a longer steering oar at the stern. By this time, they were also frequently fitted with a removable mast, sail, and rudder. For a quiet approach to a whale they could be paddled. The aim was to attach the boat to the whale with a harpoon, which had 900 feet of fine 3/4-inch manila whale line attached. The whale line was stowed in a large tub two-thirds of the way aft, with another tub forward of it containing another 900 feet of spare line that could be tied on. The whale line led from the tub back to a stout oak post called the loggerhead, near the stern, around which it was wrapped as a brake. Then it led all the way forward between the oarsmen, under a rope called the kicking strap, and through a notch at the bow, where it was tied to the principal harpoon. A second harpoon was fastened to the whale line as well, and both rested in a forked crotch on the starboard rail near the bow, ready for throwing, or darting. A boat also carried three spare harpoons in a rack.

Harpoons—or "irons" to whalemen—had evolved in the form of an arrowhead. They pierced a whale's flesh easily, but the flukes of the harpoons were prone to tearing through the flesh, setting the whale free, so both harpoons were commonly darted. The boat was also equipped with four long-shanked, razor-sharp lances to perform the actual kill by piercing the whale's heart or lungs.

At the bow, each boat was fitted with a cross timber, or thigh board, with a notch—the "clumsy cleat"—in which the harpooner could brace his thigh while darting his iron, and the "box," a small deck for the coil of line called the box warp, which gave the boatsteerer some slack line as he darted the harpoons. Also in the boat were a square wooden drogue that could be attached to the whale line as a drag to slow the whale and a flag called a waif to plant in a dead whale to claim it. For safety, each boat had a compass, a small keg of water, and a keg with a lantern as well as some hardtack (thick, hard crackers) to eat if the boat became separated from the vessel. In all, a whaleboat carried about nine hundred pounds of equipment, and the crew added nearly nine hundred pounds more.

Each of the six men in the boat had a specific function. The captain and mates acted as boatheaders, standing at the stern, steering with a long oar, and issuing commands to the five oarsmen. The boatheader would also keep an eye on the ship, watching for flag signals indicating the location of the whales, upwind, downwind, or in relation to the ship. At the bow, the boatsteerer rowed until he was ordered to rise, turn around, and dart his iron. If the whale was "gallied" (alarmed) and swimming away, the boatsteerers might throw the harpoons, but ideally the boat was brought right up to the whale and the boatsteerer drove the harpoons deeply into the whale's back. The boatheader would then command "Stern all!" to move the boat away from the "flurry" of the surprised whale—maybe a lashing of the tail, a snapping of the jaws, or simply a dash that would take the boat on a "Nantucket sleighride." As the whale line ran out, the boatsteerer made his way aft to take the steering oar: Hence, in American ships, he was commonly called boatsteerer, not harpooner. Then the boatheader hurried forward to handle the killing lance.

The aftermost oarsman pulled the stroke oar, setting the pace of the rowing as directed by the boatheader. When the boat was fast to the whale, he kept the loggerhead wet to prevent the friction of the line from setting wood and rope afire. Ahead of him sat the tub oarsman, who shared his space with a tub of whale line, which it was his duty to keep wet as the line ran out. The midship oarsman was usually the largest man in the boat and pulled the longest oar. (With three oars to starboard and two on the larboard side, their lengths varied to balance the pull.) When the boat was fast to the whale, he like the others "peaked" his oar by tucking its loom (handle end) into a cleat on the side by his thwart (seat) so the whale line would run smoothly through the vee formed by the oar shafts. He also had a tub of whale line to keep wet and added his strength in pulling the boat up on the whale line to reach the whale once it tired. Forward of him, the bow oarsman, who was probably the most experienced seaman in the boat, assisted in stepping and lowering the mast and sail and tended the whale line as the boatheader wielded his lance for the kill.

The boatheader had the honor of killing the exhausted whale with a long, sharp lance. He would probe, trying to pierce the heart or lungs, and churn his lance till the whale exhaled blood. Then he ordered the crew to "stern all" to avoid the whale's death throws—the final "flurry." When the whale rolled "fin out" on its side, the men would claim their kill.

—◦◦✕◦◦—

On September 26, the *Morgan* reached the Azores. These nine volcanic islands lie two thousand miles east of New Bedford and nine hundred miles west of Portugal. The islands were first occupied by Portuguese colonists in the 1430s, followed by Flemish settlers from what is now Belgium. Islanders engaged in both agriculture and fishing, but population pressure encouraged young island men to emigrate or to find employment as sailors on visiting vessels. For decades, American whalers had called at the Azores' principal port of Horta on the island of Faial, where the American diplomatic consul resided. There, they purchased fresh provisions and recruited island men, many of whom were skilled boatmen, to fill vacancies in the crew. Those who joined American whaleships often ended up in New Bedford, where they established a growing Azorean community. The *Morgan* spent two days tacking back and forth off Horta while each watch received a day ashore and an island boat delivered supplies.

Horta, Faial, a frequent port of call for whaleships, was depicted in the whaling panorama painted by Benjamin Russell and Caleb Purrington, ca. 1848. (IMAGE COURTESY OF THE NEW BEDFORD WHALING MUSEUM)

On September 28, Captain Norton headed the ship toward Cape Horn, seven thousand miles south at the tip of South America, on the way to the Pacific Ocean. On October 6, the ship passed the Cabo Verde Islands off Africa, another group of Atlantic islands at which New England whaleships often took on supplies and crew members. On October 13, the crew lowered the whaleboats to practice their duties, and two days later they lowered and chased some blackfish (pilot whales) without success. On November 1, as they approached Cape Horn, where strong winds and high seas swept from the Pacific to the Atlantic, the crew hoisted in the bow and waist boats to prepare for heavy seas, and for most of November they worked to windward under reefed (shortened) topsails or hove to in order to ride out the mountainous seas. Occasionally they saw right whales but could not lower to chase them. On December 4, Second Mate Osborn reported the "Watch Employed in Sawing Wood to keep from Freezing."

Once past Cape Horn, the ship steered north into the Pacific, headed for the sperm whaling grounds near the island of Mas Afuera (now Alejandro Selkirk Island, named for the marooned sailor whose time on the island may have inspired Daniel Defoe's 1719 novel, *Robinson Crusoe*). In the morning of December 13, the crew on deck sighted the ship's first sperm whales. Captain Norton and First Mate Chadwick lowered their boats in pursuit. According to Osborn's journal, "Starboard [captain's] Boat struck a Small Cow Whale the Larboard [mate's] Boat struck & drawed his iron," meaning the harpoon tore out and the whale escaped.

Then, for the first time, the crew became whale-oil processors. Having towed the whale to the *Morgan*, they lashed it along the starboard side, tail forward, with a fluke chain around the small of the body at the flukes, leading through a pipe in the bulwarks to be secured on deck.

Amidships, a ten-foot length of the starboard bulwarks could be removed to make a gangway for the cutting process. Two short platforms—which would later be replaced by a long plank cutting stage with railing—were lowered so the ship's mates could stand on them to cut up the whale with long cutting spades. First, they removed the head. With the whale on its side, jaw toward the vessel, they cut around the socket of the jaw to unhinge it. A large cutting tackle, with twenty-inch blocks, was lashed to the mainmast below the main top, and the lower block and chain strop were brought down and hooked through a hole in the flesh. The cutting tackle fall was run forward to the windlass, and the crew manned the windlass to raise the jaw on deck. The mates then cut around the head until it came free and could be lashed by chain through a hawsepipe aft of the gangway.

The mates then began to cut a diagonal incision through the blubber, producing a six-foot-wide strip that whalemen called the blanket piece. The cutting tackle was attached and, while the mates cut, the crew hoisted the blubber free of the whale until the blocks met. Then another cutting tackle was attached through the blanket piece at the rail, and the first section was cut free and lowered through the main hatch into the blubber room in the 'tween decks. The process continued diagonally around the carcass until it was stripped of blubber. The carcass—muscles, organs, and bones—was then set adrift to be consumed by sharks and sea birds.

The head was brought to the gangway, and the lower part, called the junk, was cut free, hoisted aboard, and lashed to the rail. The upper part of the head, which whalemen called the case, was then either hoisted aboard or lashed at the gangway. The case contained the spermaceti, so it was cut open and a case bucket was used to dip out the spermaceti. With a large whale, a boatsteerer or two might climb into the case to dip out the waxy liquid spermaceti. A large sperm whale could have as much as thirty barrels—almost one thousand gallons—of spermaceti. The head was then cut free, and the tryworks was prepared.

Located aft of the foremast, the tryworks was a brick furnace, with two large cast-iron pots, built over a water-filled "goose pen" that kept it from burning through the deck.

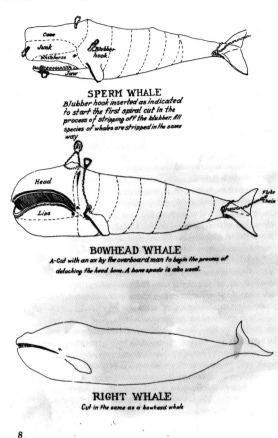

The *Charles W. Morgan*

SPERM WHALE
Blubber hook inserted as indicated to start the first spiral cut in the process of stripping off the blubber. All species of whales are stripped in the same way

BOWHEAD WHALE
A-Cut with an ax by the overboard man to begin the process of detaching the head bone. A bone spade is also used.

RIGHT WHALE
Cut in the same as a bowhead whale

8

A diagram of the way whales were "cut in." ILLUSTRATION BY JOHN F. LEAVITT. (MYSTIC SEAPORT MUSEUM, 1977-2-188)

The crew lit a wood fire in the tryworks below the pots to heat them to a boiling temperature. Below, in the blubber room, men were cutting the blanket pieces into smaller two-by-six-foot "horse pieces," which were then minced with crosscuts to fully expose the blubber. These "bible leaves" were forked into the try-pots and stirred to keep the oil that was rendered out from burning. The fleshy remnants of the blubber, called cracklings, were strained out of the try-pots and tossed in the furnaces to feed the fire. When the pots were full of oil, the crew began to ladle it into cooling tanks alongside the tryworks. The spermaceti was also heated in the tryworks to liquify it again. An average sperm whale might produce forty-five to fifty barrels of oil, while a large old "bull" could produce as much as one hundred barrels. The cooled oil was bailed into casks on deck or run through a canvas hose to the casks below. Once the oil casks were stowed in the hold and the decks were scrubbed, the hunt continued.

Officers on the *Morgan*'s cutting stage use their long-handled cutting spades to separate the case (forehead) from a dead sperm whale's head. This sequence of photographs may have been taken during the *Morgan*'s 1902–1903 voyage. (MYSTIC SEAPORT MUSEUM, 1975.383.70)

Photographed from a whaleboat, the *Morgan*'s officers on the cutting stage continue cutting in. With the oily structure called the junk cut free above the jaw, one cutting tackle supports the case while the other begins to bring the blanket piece of blubber aboard. (MYSTIC SEAPORT MUSEUM,1975.383.73)

With the junk on deck at left, the officers on the cutting stage pause as the cutting tackle is secured to the whale. The men wear foul-weather gear because a slippery mix of oil and water coats everything. (MYSTIC SEAPORT MUSEUM, 1975-1-485)

A section of the blanket piece of thick blubber is brought on board to be lowered through the main hatch into the blubber room for cutting into horse pieces. (MYSTIC SEAPORT MUSEUM, 1975.383.56)

With the blanket piece removed and the carcass set adrift, the case is hoisted aboard. (MYSTIC SEAPORT MUSEUM, 1975.383.65)

The junk (left) and case are lashed along the rail.
(MYSTIC SEAPORT MUSEUM, 1975.383.62)

Up to his waist in the case, a whaleman—possibly a boatsteerer—exchanges a bucket for spermaceti with the man at left. (MYSTIC SEAPORT MUSEUM, 1975.383.51)

With the tryworks smoking, a whaleman uses a mincing knife on the mincing horse (a cutting surface and box) to cut a horse piece brought up from the blubber room into thinly sliced "bible leaves" to render in the try-pots. At left, a whaleman stands on the scrap box, which holds "cracklings" that have rendered their oil and will be used as fuel in the tryworks. Rendered oil will be dipped into a copper cooling tank on the starboard side of the tryworks. (MYSTIC SEAPORT MUSEUM, 1975.383.89)

Right and bowhead whales were processed in a similar manner, except that only the upper jaw, with baleen fronds, was saved from the head. Here a whaleman adjusts the tackle as a bowhead jaw with its very long baleen is hoisted aboard. (MYSTIC SEAPORT MUSEUM, 1975.383.74)

Once the oil was cool enough, it was usually run through a canvas hose to fill casks in the hold. Here, the *Morgan*'s cooper sets up new casks from sets of staves called shooks. Behind him are fragments of reeds, which the whalemen called flags, that were placed between the staves to seal the seams and keep the casks tight. At left is the corner of Mrs. Tinkham's deck house, and between that and the mainmast is the companionway to steerage, where the boatsteerers and "idlers" lived. With the deck washed and scrubbed of oil, the crew has done its laundry and hung clothing to dry in the rigging. (MYSTIC SEAPORT MUSEUM, 1975.383.79)

On the day after New Year's, the *Morgan* met the ship *Nantucket* of Nantucket, which had already taken four hundred barrels of oil, and the captains got together on one of the ships to socialize in a "gam." When gamming at sea, the captain of one vessel and his boat's crew visited the other vessel, while that vessel's first mate and his boat's crew visited the first vessel. Six days later the crew gammed with their neighbors from Edgartown on the *Champion*.

"Squareheads," as whalemen called sperm whales, frequented the waters off the west coast of South America, but the boats chased them all day without success. The ship came to anchor with several other whaleships at Callao, Peru, at the beginning of February. The watches received liberty ashore while the ship resupplied with water and potatoes.

To obtain fresh water for drinking and cooking, the *Morgan* had to call at a place with a spring, river, or stream every few months. There, whaleboat crews towed casks to the water source and filled them, then towed them back and hoisted them into the hold. Each day, water was drawn from the storage casks to fill a large wooden cask with an opening in the top called a scuttlebutt. Holding about 126 gallons, the scuttlebutt was secured on deck for the use of the sailors (scuttlebutt as a term for gossip comes from the rumors sailors might share as they gathered around their water source). Since the water might be tainted by organic matter from the streams or whale oil from earlier uses of the casks, some preferred to take their water boiled as coffee, heavily sweetened with molasses.

After a week at Callao, the *Morgan* headed out, "Bound on the off Shore Ground, to look all round." But soon they headed back for Peru, calling at Paita, north of Callao, "to Land Letters & get the News." Then the ship headed north for the Galápagos Islands, taking a few blackfish along the way. At the Galápagos, the crew went ashore to capture "turpins" (tortoises) for turtle soup.

Such a rich soup was a welcome change from the usual fare. Sailors consumed a diet high in protein, fat, carbohydrates, and salt. The basic provisions were beef and pork heavily salted and packed in barrels, flour packed in barrels, and ship's bread (hardtack) packed in barrels. Each day the cook might bake sourdough bread and boil either salt beef or salt pork, then pan-fry it in its own fat. Especially when whaling off the coast of South America, he had access to a variety of potatoes for boiling. He could make soups with leftover meat and the root vegetables carried on board. For holidays, he might boil a plum duff, a flour pudding sweetened with molasses and raisins. After stopping at tropical locations, the crew would have a supply of fruit for a short period, but fruits and green vegetables were only occasional elements of their diet. They sometimes caught fish, but fresh meat and eggs were only available when the captain purchased live animals and brought them aboard.

Cruising aimlessly on the offshore grounds near the equator, Mate Osborn noted, "Saw a few half starved Porpoises. Last part fine weather & rather faint Hearted about getting Home in 28 Months." On April 17, during "glorious" weather, Osborn was thinking of home, noting, "Last part a fine Moon to Promenade the Causeway [on Martha's Vineyard]. So ends. Home Sick. Lat. 2.36—Long. 111.20." On May 2, he complained, "Whales as plenty, as they are in our Corn Fields at Home." Finally, after weeks of sighting only finback and blue whales, and lowering boats to gam with other ships rather than lowering for whales, on May 27, they "Raised a Breach about 1/2 past 8 oclock." With two pods of sperm whales in sight, they lowered all four boats. The captain's and mate's boat struck the same bull whale, which stove

the mate's boat. But the starboard boat held on and killed the whale, which was brought to the ship and cut in to produce twenty-six barrels of oil.

The next day, Osborn's waist boat took a thirty-eight-barrel bull sperm whale, "the first for me." A few days later, on June 3, the starboard boat lost its whale, the larboard boat cut its line while lancing its whale, and the bow and waist boats struck and killed the same whale. After towing it to the ship, they were "almost buffed out." It was a one-hundred-barrel sperm whale, the teeth of which weighed eighty-five pounds.

After the crew had filled the available casks with oil, the ship's cooper began to assemble additional casks from bundles of oak staves called shooks. As he set the staves in their hoops, he placed strips of dried reed (phragmites) called flags between the staves to seal the seams. Once the crew had maneuvered the full casks of oil into place in the hold, the cooper would check them periodically. If they showed signs of drying and leaking, he would have them soaked down with sea water so the wood would swell. When the crew

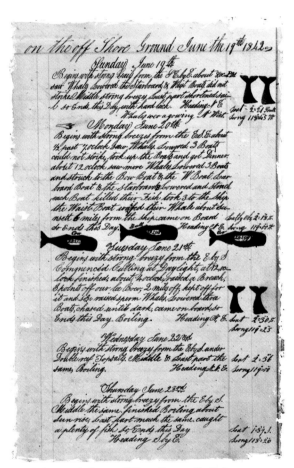

In his journal, Second Mate James C. Osborn recorded five busy days of whaling on the "off shore ground" in June 1842. Mates often used carved ivory or wood stamps to document encounters with whales. The tail-up symbols indicate whales that escaped. The profile stamps, shaped to represent the different species of whale, have a space to note the number of barrels of oil the whale produced. (MYSTIC SEAPORT MUSEUM, LOG 143)

used the bilge pumps aft of the mainmast to pump out this water, plus any that had leaked into the ship, they kept the bilge fresh.

Heading back to Peru, the ship stopped again at the Galapágos Islands, where whalers sometimes left mail for other ships or to be carried home. Along the coast and off the islands, one of the mates would sometimes climb down to the chain stays under the bowsprit with the ship's five-prong "grains" to spear mahi-mahi and other fish to supplement the crew's diet. After calling at the supply port of Paita again, the ship headed up the coast to Tumbes (Tombez to the whalemen) to obtain fresh water, potatoes, and firewood. There, the crews of fourteen other whaleships gathered aboard the *Morgan* to socialize. When the musical instruments came out on that crowded deck, they had a real "breakdown," or dance.

Back at sea, the ship had good luck, taking six whales on November 17. In April 1843, the ship took three whales in one day, and the next day the crew was busy "Boiling [oil] and Frying Dough Nuts." It was already a tradition of American whaling crews to celebrate stowing one thousand barrels of oil with the cook frying dough balls in the whale oil in the tryworks.

In May 1843, the ship's luck changed. "Last Part Dreary & Gloomy, Sorrowful and Home Sick, Sea Sick and Sick of the Sea, Amen, and it is 26 days since we have seen a whale," lamented Osborn. With plenty of sperm whale teeth on board and a more leisurely pace, some of the men took up "scrimshoning"—carving them into decorative implements or incising them with pictures. Captain Norton had offered to teach navigation to anyone who wished to learn the use of the octant or sextant in finding the angle of the sun or stars overhead and the calculations needed to convert those angles to a position on the ocean. About twenty of the crew took the chance to learn a skill that would allow them to serve as an officer, and at least two of them—twenty-year-old Nathan M. Jernegan and seventeen-year-old John A. Luce—would rise through the ranks to command whaleships.

As they cruised the offshore ground, where whales were scarce, Osborn noted, "Employed a schrimshon" and "Nothing remarkable only Dancing." On June 16,

1843, he recorded, "Strong southeast trades . . . middle part about 12 o'clock a man fell overboard. The ship was luffed to the wind and a boat lowered in about two shakes. One of the boatsteerers fastened to him solid and we sterned all out of the suds. He was about 1/4 mile from the ship when we got him. His name is Norton." William R. Norton of Edgartown, a distant relative of Captain Norton, had begun the voyage as a fifteen-year-old greenhand.

After calling at rugged Cocos Island, several hundred miles northeast of the Galápagos, for fresh water in July, they took a whale on the way to Tumbes, where "the old man" (captain) went ashore to confirm the rumors of a fever "a rageing up & down the Coast." At Paita, at the beginning of August, two of the crew deserted and First Mate Charles Chadwick was discharged for illness. Osborn went "a visiting the Ladyes, on board the Ship George of Fare Haven. A good spree and no mistake."

Again the ship cruised the grounds off South America with little luck. One day in December, after killing roaches in the fo'c'sle, all hands went for a swim. At Paita in February 1844, where the crew was given liberty on shore, Captain Norton discharged the carpenter and another man for sickness and signed on three new men. One was Henry Dally, a sailor who personified the wandering nature of sea-farers. Dally claimed to be the son of a New York sailmaker and an apprentice to another New York sailmaker. He ran away at eighteen and joined the New Bedford whaleship *Winslow* in 1833. Finding the bad food and severe discipline too much to bear, he deserted at Cocos Island. He then spent a couple of years on another whaleship before landing in Paita. After several short whaling voyages, he signed aboard a Nantucket vessel and returned to New England, visiting his family for the first time in years. Back at sea, he ended up sick in the Azores. When he recovered, he joined another whaleship, which deposited him on the east coast of Africa. At

Whaleships fill the anchorage at Lahaina, Maui, in this detail from the whaling panorama painted by Benjamin Russell and Caleb Purrington, ca. 1848. (IMAGE COURTESY OF THE NEW BEDFORD WHALING MUSEUM)

A crowd of whaleships works the Northwest Coast waters off Alaska in this detail from the whaling panorama painted by Benjamin Russell and Caleb Purrington, ca. 1848. The vessel at right hoists the upper jaw of a right whale with its long fronds of baleen while the vessel at center hoists a blanket piece of blubber. The vessels at left have their tryworks smoking as they process oil. Whaleboats chase right whales in the foreground. (IMAGE COURTESY OF THE NEW BEDFORD WHALING MUSEUM)

Mozambique, he worked briefly as a sailmaker before signing aboard a Spanish slaving vessel for a passage to Havana. After a trading voyage between Havana and Africa, he returned to New York, then signed aboard the New Bedford whaleship *Pacific* in 1837. Two years later, he left the ship in Peru and worked briefly as a sailmaker in Guayaquil, Ecuador, before joining a coasting vessel. He then served briefly on another whaler but left it at Paita to avoid a cold season in the North Pacific. He then signed aboard the *Morgan* when it arrived at Paita.

After a stop at Tumbes for potatoes and firewood, the ship cruised west, then set a course for the Hawaiian Islands, which had been settled by Polynesian canoe voyagers before the year 1000 and "discovered" by Captain James Cook in 1778. The peoples of the independent islands were united between 1795 and 1810 by King Kamehameha I, who established the Hawaiian Kingdom. He settled the capital of the kingdom at Lahaina on the west coast of the island of Maui, but Honolulu, on the island of Oahu, northwest of Maui, was growing as a commercial port and would become the capital in 1850. American whalers first visited the islands in about 1820, the year Christian missionaries from New England began to arrive. As the crossroads of the Pacific, these islands gave whaleships an idyllic place to resupply, to obtain information from the merchant and whaling ships that called there, and even to ship whale oil home aboard those ships. For the sailors, access to alcohol and to island women, with their approach to sexuality, casual by European

and American standards, made the islands a popular stop, even as the missionaries attempted to impose more temperate behavior.

On April 4, the *Morgan* anchored at the whalers' principal port of Lahaina, joining twenty-five other whaleships there. When the vessel departed for Honolulu on April 8, it carried eight passengers, including the transplanted Boston mariner and merchant Charles Brewer and his wife and five "Dear little Yellow Girls" as passengers.

From Honolulu, Captain Norton directed the ship toward the increasingly popular whaling grounds on the Northwest Coast in the Gulf of Alaska. After a stormy passage during which Mate Osborn's waist boat was smashed, or "stove," in its davits by the sea, the ship was on the grounds by May 1 and began to sight right whales all around the ship. On May 5, Osborn was injured when the ship's stern struck him while they were lowering boats: "Snowing hard and hard luck for me," he wrote.

In his journal, Second Mate Osborn drew a sperm whale towing a whaleboat as the mate at the bow prepares to lance it. He titled his sketch "A Regular Botch." Note the dark paint scheme of the boat. (MYSTIC SEAPORT MUSEUM, LOG 143)

After three weeks of futilely chasing whales, having the whale line part, or being constrained by wind or fog, the larboard boat finally "struck" (harpooned) and killed a 150-barrel right whale on May 24.

With a right whale alongside, they first separated the head and hoisted it aboard to strip the fronds of baleen from the upper jaw before setting the head adrift and cutting in the rest of the whale in the same manner as a sperm whale. After cutting in and having dinner, they "set the Try Works a Smoaking" and spent the next day trying out, or rendering, the oil. Thereafter, about once a week they got a 150-barrel whale. On July 2, when the waist boat took a 240-barrel right whale, Osborn noted, "you want from 5 to 6 foot lances" to reach the whale's lungs through all that blubber. On July 8, they salvaged a "Stinking Dead Whale" and tried out sixty barrels of oil from its decaying blubber.

On July 17, in the vicinity of Kodiak Island, Captain Norton set a course for Monterey in Mexico's Upper California. But whaling continued, and, on August 5, they took three sperm whales. When whaling was slow, they scraped any remaining flesh off the baleen and spread it around the deck and lower rigging to dry, then bundled it for storage below deck. Coming to anchor at Monterey on August 10, the watches went ashore "to grass." The next day, with the starboard watch ashore, the larboard boat was launched and took a seventeen-barrel humpback whale in the harbor. While the ship lay there, Henry Dally and three other men, including two Pacific islanders, were discharged. Dally would be one of the early US settlers in California.

With a fresh supply of water and firewood, the ship hoisted anchor "with a good will" on August 18 for the passage south. The crew tuned up the rigging on the way to Cape Horn, which they passed on October 27. During their 1,211-day voyage, the crew had sighted sperm whales fifty-one times and taken fifty-nine whales that produced 1,950 barrels of oil by the time they performed the tradition of "Heaving the Try Works Overboard" on December 11. Among all the ship's work they were called to do in the voyage's last days, they were "employed Scrimshoning the Monkey Rail" at the ship's stern.

———◦◦◇◦◦———

Having made the fourteen-thousand-mile passage from Monterey in a short 130 days, the *Charles W. Morgan* anchored off New Bedford on January 2, 1845. When the New Bedford Harbor pilot came on board to bring the ship safely into port, he brought along a temperance pledge likely sponsored by the port's temperance society. A sailor's benevolent publication reported that every member of the crew signed it.

According to Charles W. Morgan, the ship had produced 33,394.5 gallons (256 casks) of sperm oil and 14,387.5 gallons of head matter (spermaceti) worth $.85 per gallon; 25,835.5 gallons (226 casks) of right-whale oil worth $.54 per gallon; 2,129 gallons of less desirable dark oil valued at $.31 per gallon; 8,900 pounds of "whalebone" (baleen) worth $.33 a pound; and 48 pounds of "scaldings" worth $.55 per pound. The cargo's total value amounted to $54,686 (about $2,188,500 in 2023). From this, Morgan deducted $1,783 to cover the 2.5 percent commission due the owners, plus the fees for pilotage (bringing the ship into harbor), wharfage (the cost of space at the wharf), gauging the quantity of oil with special measuring tools, coopering the casks to keep them tight on shore, resupplying the ship's medicine chest, and cleaning the ship.

For his 1/15th lay, Captain Norton received $3,417.92 (almost $137,000 in 2023), plus a share as an owner and a share of the sale of "slops"—tobacco, clothing, and necessities—sold to the crew during the voyage. Second Mate Osborn's 1/45th lay returned him $1,139, Steward Manuel Lopez's 1/125th lay was worth $410.15, and a greenhand's "long" 1/180th lay equaled $284.83 (about $11,400 in 2023). But their shares were reduced by deductions for the money and clothing advanced to them at the beginning of the voyage (calculated at thirty percent of their estimated return), interest and insurance on those advances, and interest on the slops they drew onboard and on money advanced to them during the voyage. Steward Manuel Lopez also had to pay interest on the $50 advanced to his wife in New Bedford during his absence.

In an oil works, the sperm-whale oil was boiled to evaporate any water, then frozen, and finally pressed at different temperatures and with different tonnages to produce different qualities of oil. The solid material that remained was spermaceti, which was further processed and molded into candles. (MYSTIC SEAPORT MUSEUM, 1995.291)

The *Morgan's* oil was unloaded on the wharf, where a gauger—perhaps part-owner David Brayton—used a measuring rod to calculate the volume of each cask. The casks were commonly lined up on the wharves and covered with seaweed to keep them moist, because the processing of the oil usually took place in winter. At the oil works, the oil and spermaceti were mixed and boiled in try-pots for about ten hours to evaporate any remaining water. Any solids left in the oil were skimmed off to be used in soap. Then the oil was frozen in fifty-gallon chunks. The frozen oil was pressed under a ton of weight to produce the finest-quality "winter oil," which remained liquid below freezing. The remnants—about a third of the total—were pressed at fifty degrees temperature to produce "spring oil." The remainder was heated to eighty degrees and pressed under fifty tons of weight to produce the lowest quality "taut pressed oil." The remaining solid mass was spermaceti, which was heated with caustic soda to whiten it and then formed into fine, white, clean-burning candles.

—◦◦◇◇◦◦—

Charles W. Morgan had five months to settle his accounts and prepare his ship for the next voyage. This time the *Morgan* would be crewed by a typical mix of men from many origins, rather than the largely homogeneous crew of the previous voyage. For captain, Morgan obtained the services of forty-two-year-old John D. Samson of New Bedford, who had commanded whaleships since the 1820s. First Mate William Clement, thirty, came from Philadelphia, and other crew members were originally from Upstate New York. Two men from the first voyage, Wampanoag Zenas Gould and seaman Abraham Weaver, now promoted to boatsteerer, would sail again.

The ship departed on June 10, and nine days later the crew took its first sperm whale. Captain Samson was largely confined to his cabin by a leg ailment, but the crew felt his strict discipline. He prohibited both card playing and fighting on board, and in August he threatened to flog one man for fighting.

In the South Atlantic in September, the ship stopped at the island of Tristan da Cunha for supplies. Though sighted and named by Portuguese explorers as early as 1506, Tristan da Cunha and its outer islands were not settled until 1810. Annexed by Great Britain, the island became a supply depot for whaleships, and some of its young men obtained employment on American whaleships. When the *Morgan* left Tristan, the deck resembled a barnyard, with a bullock, six sheep, six hogs, eighteen chickens, six turkeys, and four geese. These would supplement the preserved food during the nearly nine-thousand-mile run across the Indian Ocean to the sperm-whaling grounds off New Zealand.

During that passage, when two men got into a fight, Captain Samson imposed old-style shipboard discipline, as practiced in the US Navy. "The Captain had them called aft and seized up in the presence of the ship's company, when the Captain gave them one dozen [lashes] apiece with a piece of [moderately heavy] 15 thread rattling stuff, when they were cast off and let go." Tied with their hands in the rigging and lashed on the back with a small rope in front of their fellow sailors, the culprits suffered both pain and humiliation, and their fellows received a further warning against misbehavior. Despite the growth of social reform movements, corporal punishment remained legal aboard American ships, although it would be prohibited aboard Navy ships in 1850.

In February 1846, the *Morgan* reached the Bay of Islands on the northeast coast of New Zealand's North Island. There, six men promptly deserted. The ship then headed northeast for the sperm-whaling grounds near Fiji, Samoa, and Tonga. In May, Captain Samson broke whaling etiquette when he came forward and entered the fo'c'sle to search for and confiscate the crew's playing cards.

Two months later, the ship arrived at Apia in the Navigator Islands (Samoa). There, Captain Samson discharged two men with the pay that was due them: 132.5 gallons of oil apiece. Later, the captain gave a lashing to a sailor who was often unfit for duty because the mercury he took for his venereal disease made him sick. The sailor would finally desert two years later.

The crew remained unhappy even as they had luck in taking whales. Men deserted or were discharged at every island where the ship called for provisions. Captain Samson replaced them with a mix of stranded American seamen and Native Pacific Islanders—"Kanakas" as the whalemen called them, using the Hawaiian word for "people" or "human beings."

In June 1847, at Rotuma, Fiji, Captain Samson purchased fifteen casks of whale oil from a wrecked ship in exchange for five muskets. For the next four months the ship cruised without sighting a whale. The discord continued aboard, and one of the men talked back to the first mate, then grappled with the captain and mates. They tied him up for three hours and struck him with a rope's end.

At Vava'u, Tonga, Captain Samson filled the ship's deck with forty-six hogs and eighty fowl. He then headed the ship back to the Bay of Islands. The *Morgan* finally began the return journey to New Bedford in the summer of 1848. While the ship was still a month out in the Atlantic, the chronometer broke, leaving the captain and mate without an accurate timepiece with which to make their navigation calculations. But they found their way home, arriving on December 9, 1848.

While it had been a contentious voyage, it turned out to be a profitable one. "The ship has 2100 bbls Sperm oil & 100 bbls whale oil on board and sent home 70 bbl sperm oil, a good voyage, and in good time for me at any rate," wrote Charles W. Morgan in his diary. "I shall be able to pay off some of my notes & lessen my liabilities to the banks.—Sperm oil is high worth perhaps 108 to 110 cts per gall." In the end, Morgan calculated the return at $75,011.09 (about $2,888,000 in 2023). Morgan's 7/16 share paid him $23,131.26, while Captain Samson's 1/16 lay was worth $4,535.45. After two voyages and seven years, the *Charles W. Morgan* had returned almost five times its building cost.

CHAPTER 4

Charles W. Morgan Sells His Namesake

1849-1863

Although he felt strongly about his namesake vessel, Charles W. Morgan ultimately was forced to make a hard decision. During the ship's absence in the southwestern Pacific, the United States and Mexico had gone to war in 1846, and, by the Treaty of Guadalupe Hidalgo in early 1848, the United States annexed more than half a million square miles of land and extended the nation's border to the California coast. Even before the treaty was signed, gold had been discovered in the foothills of California's Sierra Nevada mountains, news of which reached the East Coast that summer. By the end of 1848, eager "argonauts" were

PHOTO BY ANDY PRICE. (MYSTIC SEAPORT MUSEUM, D2014-06-0924)

SHIP CHARLES W. MORGAN FOR SALE.

The fine, fast sailing Ship CHARLES W MOR-
GAN is offered for sale. This Ship was built in 1841
by the M ssrs. Hillman, burthen 351 tons, entirely
copper fastened outside to the rail—thoroughly salted on
the stocks, and re-salted since. She is a very fast sailer,
and can be sent to sea in two weeks. Apply to
feb 8 tf   CHAS. W. MORGAN, Rotch's wharf.

Charles W. Morgan advertised his namesake ship for sale in the *New Bedford Daily Mercury* **in February 1849. He emphasized that the ship was "a very fast sailer," thoroughly fastened with durable copper spikes and packed with salt between the frames to prevent rot from freshwater seepage.** (MYSTIC SEAPORT MUSEUM)

buying ships of all types to carry them and their supplies to the new port of San Francisco (formerly the settlement of Yerba Buena). With the market for ships suddenly inflated, Morgan decided to offer the *Charles W. Morgan* for sale.

Describing the ship as very well built and "a very fast sailer," he offered it for $18,000 (about $713,000 in 2023). A buyer from Boston responded at the end of January 1849, and Morgan noted, "She was sold by the Telegraph all within an hour—offer and answer." Yet the transaction fell apart, and it was more than a month before Morgan would write on March 8, "this day sold the principal part of Ship C.W. Morgan to Edwd Mott Robinson at the rate of $17000 to be fitted for whaling—reserving 1/8 for myself and 1/8 for Francis Rotch—This was an unpleasant matter but being determined to retrench my business, I did not hesitate."

A few years younger than Charles W. Morgan, Edward Mott Robinson was also a Quaker born in Philadelphia who had married into a New Bedford whaling family, becoming a partner in the port's largest whaling firm, Isaac Howland Jr. & Company. He would also become a partner in William T. Coleman & Company, which began fast clipper-ship service between New York and San Francisco in response to the gold rush. Like Morgan, Robinson served as a director of a bank and an insurance company and invested in cotton mills.

Despite his developing interest in the California trade, Robinson did not pack the *Charles W. Morgan* with supplies and passengers and send it to San Francisco, where it likely would have been abandoned in the bay as hundreds of ships were. Rather, he simply readied the *Morgan* for another whaling voyage and retained John D. Samson as captain. Thacher Packard of Sandwich, Massachusetts, possibly a boatsteerer during the last voyage—was now first mate, and William Griffin, originally of Waterloo, New York, had risen from third to second mate. The rest of the crew was new. One of the new boatsteerers, Nelson Cole Haley, was an eighteen-year-old acquaintance of the captain. Haley later wrote out

Nelson Cole Haley (1832–1900) joined the *Morgan* as an eighteen-year-old boatsteerer in 1849. His manuscript reminiscences are the only account of the 1849–1853 voyage. Here he poses with his wife Charlotte Brown Haley, probably in the 1860s. (MYSTIC SEAPORT MUSEUM, 1948.52)

his reminiscences of the voyage in a manuscript that his descendants donated to Mystic Seaport Museum in the 1940s. Published under the title *Whale Hunt*, it is the only account of this voyage.

On June 5, 1849, Captain Samson took the *Morgan* out of New Bedford for another voyage across the Indian Ocean to the Bay of Islands, New Zealand. From there, the ship again cruised the western Pacific sperm-whaling grounds as far north as the equator. As on the previous voyage, the ship called repeatedly at islands caught in a long cultural clash between islanders and the American and European vessels that arrived carrying whalers, traders, and Christian missionaries. While the missionaries tried to convert the islanders from their own religions, whalemen took advantage of them, trading fabric and trinkets for livestock and provisions, and sometimes the use of island women. They also lured island men to fill vacancies in the crew, lumping them all as "Kanakas," often renaming them with English names, and treating them as a homeless population of maritime laborers, who were paid in a foreign (to them) currency and rarely returned to their home islands.

Too frequently, contact with the islands led to exploitation and domination, followed by retribution from the proud islanders. According to Haley, at the atoll of Nonouti (Sydenham) in the Gilbert (formerly Kingsmill) Islands, more than one thousand miles north of Fiji, the *Morgan* drifted in close to the long reef. When many islanders approached in their canoes, threatening the ship, the crew lined the rail, armed with a few firearms as well as the ship's sharp whaling lances and cutting spades. The natives attempted to climb aboard but were repulsed. The current carried the ship past the reef, and, when a breeze arose, the *Morgan* sailed away safely.

On August 20, 1851, somewhere to the east of the *Morgan*'s position, the whale-ship *Ann Alexander* lost two boats to an aggressive sperm whale. The whale then turned on the ship, ramming it hard enough to shatter planks and sink it, leaving the crew in their boats for two days until another whaleship rescued them. Three months later, a book titled *Moby-Dick or, the Whale*, appeared in the United States. This epic novel of the fanatical hunt for a great white bull sperm whale, which includes all that the author knew about whales and whaling, ends with the whale sinking the ship and its obsessed Captain Ahab. The author, Herman Melville, had begun his brief whaling career aboard the Fairhaven bark *Acushnet* in January 1841, eventually deserting at Nuku Hiva in the Marquesas in the summer of 1842. The *Acushnet* worked the same grounds off South America hunted by the *Morgan* during its first voyage, and, during a gam with a Nantucket vessel, Melville obtained a book describing the sinking of the Nantucket whaler *Essex* by a whale in those waters in 1820. This attack resulted in an open-boat ordeal, with only eight of the twenty men surviving after being driven to cannibalism. Melville was also influenced by the 1839 account of Mocha Dick, an albino bull sperm whale reported in legend to have destroyed numerous whaleboats near Mocha Island off the coast of Chile between 1810 and his killing in about 1830. When Melville heard of the loss of the *Ann Alexander*, he remarked, "I wonder if my evil art has raised this monster." But, before and after Melville's tale, other whales would sink whaleships, either accidentally or by intention. The *Harmony* went down in 1796, and a whale rammed and sank the Nantucket whaler *Union* in 1807. Several British whalers were sunk by whales, and, as late as 1904, a whale would sink the bark *Kathleen*, making at least seven whaleships dispatched by their quarry.

After three years of cruising, with periodic returns to the Bay of Islands, Captain Samson headed back toward New Bedford with about half the take of his previous voyage. With just 1,121 barrels of oil on board, the *Morgan* arrived at New Bedford on May 27, 1853. The cargo was calculated to be worth $44,138.75 (about $1,748,777 in 2023). For his nearly four years on board, Nelson Cole Haley would receive only about $400 as his share. After deductions for the outfit provided him at the beginning of the voyage and small cash advances he received, Haley came away with just $200 (about $7,900 in 2023). After this, Haley moved to the woods of Minnesota but then returned to the sea, serving as first mate of several whaleships and, according to family legend, commanding whaleships after settling in the Hawaiian Islands.

Captain Tristram P. Ripley (1821–1881) of Edgartown, Martha's Vineyard. Captain Ripley's wife gave birth to a daughter after he departed on the *Charles W. Morgan*. The captain never saw her, as she died at age ten months. (COURTESY OF THE MARTHA'S VINEYARD MUSEUM)

For the *Morgan*'s next voyage, Robinson's firm, Isaac Howland Jr. & Company, acted as the ship's agent. The company fitted out the ship with a whole new crew and a new destination. As captain they selected Tristram P. Ripley, thirty-two, of Edgartown, Martha's Vineyard, who had risen from greenhand to master and had recently returned with the Edgartown whaler *Champion*. He had four months ashore between voyages to spend with his wife Eliza. Some months after he departed, she would give birth to their daughter Sarah. Captain Ripley would never meet her; she died when just ten months old. However, Ripley brought his thirteen-year-old nephew Benjamin along as cabin boy.

Another Edgartown mariner, Ariel Norton, signed on as second mate. Norton would eventually rise to captain and was in command of the whaleship *Awashonks* when she was crushed in the ice during the disastrous season in the Arctic Ocean on the coast of Alaska in 1871. Two brothers from Falmouth, Cape Cod, Samuel F. and Alvin H. Davis also joined the *Morgan*, at least one of them as boatsteerer.

The Howlands also had a new task for the ship: concentrating on the right whales and their relatives the bowheads of the North Pacific. American whalemen had found the dense summer population of right whales in the Gulf of Alaska in the 1830s, and the *Morgan* had made one cruise there in 1844 during its first sperm-whaling voyage. In 1847, whalemen had discovered the bowheads of the Sea of Okhotsk, north of Japan between Siberia and the Kamchatka Peninsula. Then, in 1848, Captain Thomas Welcome Roys opened a new whaling ground when he sailed into the Bering Strait between Alaska and Siberia, finding great numbers of bowhead whales there. Although the Arctic Ocean off the coast of Alaska would be the most heavily hunted region for the next fifty years, the *Morgan* would never enter the Bering Strait or whale off northwest Alaska, but the ship would chase bowheads in the Sea of Okhotsk.

In 1850, whalemen killed more than two thousand bowheads in the Bering Strait. That October, the *Honolulu Friend* newspaper published a letter, likely written by a whaleman, that was remarkable in its time for taking the whales' perspective on their slaughter: "Our enemies have wondered at our mild and inoffensive conduct; we have heard them cry, 'there she blows,' and our hearts have quailed as we saw their glittering steel reflecting the sun beams, and realized that in a few moments our life-blood oozing out, would discolor the briny deep in which we have gamboled for scores of years." He suggested, "We polar whales are a quiet inoffensive race, desirous of life and peace, but, alas, we fear our doom is sealed; we have heard the threat that in one season more we shall all be 'cut up,' and 'tried out.' Is there no redress?" He concluded, "I write in behalf of my butchered dying species. I appeal to the friends of the whole race of whales. Must we all be murdered in cold blood? Must our race become extinct?"

Adapted to life in the icy northern seas, the bowhead has extremely thick blubber for insulation and a massive skull for breaking through the ice to breathe. It has the largest mouth of any creature, measuring one-third of its body length, with baleen fronds of ten feet and more to strain out its copepod meals. Like right whales, bowheads grow to over fifty feet in length and weigh as much as 160,000 pounds. Slow swimming, highly vocal, and largely solitary, the bowhead is thought to have a natural lifespan of up to two hundred years.

For this voyage, the Howlands were speculating on the expanding market for right and bowhead oil and especially for the long fronds of baleen from their mouths. Called "whalebone" by the whalemen, this keratin material (with a composition similar to that of the human fingernail) had an increasing number of uses for strong, flexible items, from buggy whips to corset stays and more, that would later be made from petroleum-based plastics.

Departing on September 20, 1853, the *Morgan* first crossed the Atlantic to Flores in the Azores to take on fresh provisions and additional crew. The ship then headed south and was on the old whaling grounds off the Rio de la Plate above Argentina when another ship encountered it in December. The *Morgan* then rounded Cape Horn and worked northwest to resupply at Lahaina, Maui, in the Hawaiian Islands in April 1854. From there, it headed northwest to the Sea of Okhotsk to spend the summer in the foggy, ice-strewn waters there, where perhaps one hundred other whaleships cruised each summer. Between 1847 and 1857, these vessels would take almost fifteen thousand bowheads.

Bowhead whales were processed in the same way as right whales. Having no spermaceti, their foreheads were ignored. But the head was cut free so the baleen could be cut away from the upper jaw. The blubber was cut in and tried out in the usual manner, and the baleen was scraped clean of flesh, dried, and packed in bundles. A large bowhead could produce as much as 350 barrels of oil. During the summer, the *Morgan*'s crew took at least twelve whales and tried out 800 barrels of oil.

Back at Lahaina, Captain Ripley shipped home 10,700 pounds of baleen and outfitted the ship for a long cruise westward through the sperm-whaling grounds along the equator and in the Sea of Japan before arriving back in the Sea of Okhotsk when the ice went out at the beginning of summer. When the *Morgan* returned to Lahaina in the fall, it had a full cargo and was prepared for the passage home around Cape Horn. The *Morgan* arrived at New Bedford on April 27, 1856, with 12,000 pounds of baleen, 1,958 barrels of whale oil, and 268 barrels of sperm-whale oil. The value of the cargo was calculated at $76,183.64 (about $2,740,000 in 2023).

Shortly before the ship arrived back in New Bedford, Charles W. Morgan wrote Edward Mott Robinson to remind him that, before the *Morgan* sailed, Robinson had agreed to sell the ship back to Morgan once it returned. "As I built the ship and she is named for me—and as I always regretted selling her and have a wish to leave her in my family—it would gratify me to repurchase her," he wrote. Robinson told Morgan that he would exchange the ship for a vessel of comparable value, but Morgan had no ship to offer, so he never reclaimed his namesake vessel.

—◦◇◇◇◦—

In 1846—the year the Wamsutta Mills was chartered to introduce textile manufacturing to New Bedford—the American whaling fleet, representing thirty-seven ports, had reached its peak of 735 vessels, large and small, with an aggregate tonnage (cargo volume) of almost 235,000 tons and a value of $21,075,000 (more than $830,000,000 in 2023). The fleet employed almost twenty thousand men. Although the industry then began a slow contraction, its most profitable year was 1853, when the fleet landed $11,000,000 (about $43,500,000 in 2023) in whale products. New Bedford merchants would continue to invest, building the port's whaling fleet to a high of 329 vessels—fifty-five percent of the US fleet—in 1857.

That year, 105 whaling vessels would return to the port, the largest number in any year. But their arrival coincided with a national economic collapse, the Panic of 1857, which was only one of the changing currents in the whaling industry. As the price of sperm oil had increased into the 1850s, the US Lighthouse Establishment had ceased its purchases, switching first to colza (rapeseed) oil and then to coal oil for its lighthouse lanterns. Sperm oil would reach a high of $1.81 a gallon in 1855, before plunging to $1.20 in 1858.

Also in 1857, the New England–financed Pennsylvania Rock Oil Company sent Edwin Drake to prospect for crude oil in western Pennsylvania. In 1859, Drake struck oil at Titusville, which resulted in an oil boom. Within ten years, the region was producing four million barrels of petroleum a year. Refiners would determine how to distill petroleum for different uses, but they already knew how to produce light, clean-burning kerosene. In 1860, with sperm oil at $1.40 a gallon and kerosene only $.75, the transition to petroleum for illumination in homes and lighthouses was foretold.

As the Howlands outfitted the *Charles W. Morgan* in the summer of 1856, thirty-eight-year-old Thomas N. Fisher of Edgartown took command and Samuel F. Davis returned as second mate. For this voyage, the crew included four African Americans: Third Mate David Carrington, thirty-four, from Newburgh, New York; cook Henry Francis, thirty-eight, from Fishkill, New York; Smith Rowland, twenty-eight, of Lyme, Connecticut; and James Hamlin, twenty-eight, who was born to free Black parents in Norfolk, Virginia.

As an American ship's officer, David Carrington was an exception in the 1850s. Since the 1830s, American society had become more divided over race, and Black seafarers, who were once valued as sailors, were increasingly confined by restrictive laws in the South and prejudice among the agents, or "crimps," who hired crews in the North. Now, except in the whaling fleet, they were largely relegated to the positions of cook and steward, or excluded altogether. Earlier, Paul Cuffe and his family, Absolom F. Boston, Pardon Cook, and a few other African Americans had commanded whaleships, but even African American mates were unusual by the 1850s. The whaling fleet did include more than three thousand African Americans before 1860. However, the decline is evident in the fact that the proportion of New Bedford's Black population who went to sea had dropped from thirty-five percent in 1836 to just fifteen percent in 1856.

It is ironic, then, that in 1856 the *Charles W. Morgan* signed on more African American men than on any other voyage, for that was the year that violence broke out over slavery in Kansas, and just months before the Supreme Court proclaimed in the Dred Scott decision that African Americans could not be citizens. And the voyage would end six months before John Brown's raid brought the nation closer to sectional confrontation and civil war over slavery.

Steward John Raphael and cabin boy Antonio Sabina rounded out the multicultural makeup of the ship's afterguard. As before, the *Charles W. Morgan* departed in September, heading for the Azores, where Antonio de Madeiros and Jose Miguel joined the crew. The ship then headed south around Cape Horn on the way to Lahaina, Hawaii. Restocked with provisions there, the ship then headed for the Sea of Okhotsk to spend the summer hunting right and bowhead whales before returning to Hawaii in the fall. In December 1857, as the ship visited the sperm-whaling grounds of the central Pacific, the officers discovered that the ship's bread (hardtack) was moldy and the flour was wormy.

Captain Fisher maintained strict discipline. When the ship called at Ascension Island—now Pohnpei—northeast of Papua New Guinea, on the way toward the Sea of Japan in early 1858, Captain Fisher was one of very few whaling captains there who forbade prostitutes on board ship. He did, however, sign on three islanders for the crew: Tom Ascension, Friday Ascension, and Joe Ascension.

Samuel F. Davis (1833–1893) of Cape Cod served as a boatsteerer on the 1853–1856 voyage and as second mate for the 1856–1859 voyage. He later commanded several whaleships. He was photographed at New Bedford in about 1865.
(MYSTIC SEAPORT MUSEUM, 1987.66.2)

The *Morgan* entered the Sea of Japan in April, and the next month Captain Fisher flogged two men for fighting. During the summer, the crew faced foggy, rainy weather for five of every eight days. They took three small whales in Shantar Bay (now Shantar Sea) along the Siberian coast, but they found little in Southwest Bay during six weeks of hunting. With several desertions and discharges for illness in Hawaii, Captain Fisher engaged six men there for "cruise and home" seasonal work, making one or two cruises to the Sea of Okhotsk, and then paid them off back in Hawaii. He also elevated the Black cook, Henry Francis, to boatsteerer in the fall of 1858.

The ship departed Honolulu in November 1858 and arrived back in New Bedford on April 16, 1859. Despite the frustrations of the last season in the Sea of Okhotsk, the cargo produced a respectable value of $62,700 (about $2,305,000 in 2023).

———◇◇◇◇◇———

The Howland firm again secured a new captain for the next voyage. James A. Hamilton, thirty-two, had been born in Ohio but grew up in rural Connecticut before going to sea at eighteen, in 1844, as a greenhand in a whaleship from Sag Harbor, New York. His first command was in 1855; this would be his second. He was later described as "somewhat gruff in manner, but large-hearted and whole-souled." His officers and crew were a mix of men from Massachusetts, Maine, Connecticut, New York, and beyond, and, when the *Morgan* departed on October 4, he took the ship to the Azores to complete the crew.

Because sperm whales often swam through Azorean waters, in the 1850s some Azorean whalemen drew on their experience in American whaleships to establish an island whaling industry. The island of Pico was their "ship," and, when whales were sighted from the heights, they launched their boats from the beach for the hunt. Beginning with New England whaleboats, equipment, and techniques, they would eventually adapt the process and especially the boats to suit local conditions. While young Azorean greenhands might still join New England whaleships, the Azores could now offer experienced men to New England whaleships, and Azorean men could apply their whaling skills at home.

From the Azores, the *Morgan* headed for Cape Horn. In the South Atlantic, the first whales were sighted on November 30. They took one whale, but, when the waist boat struck its whale, Francis Laycock got caught in the line and was pulled out of the boat. The crew quickly cut the line to save him, but he was dead when they got him to the surface.

After rounding Cape Horn in January, the *Morgan* anchored at Talcahuano, Chile, on February 21, 1860, to obtain water and supplies. There, nine of the crew decided they had had enough of the hardships of whaling, forfeited their lays, and deserted. This was now typical among whaling crews, which were increasingly drawn

Captain James A. Hamilton (1826–1892) was born in Ohio but grew up in Connecticut. He went to sea as an eighteen-year-old greenhand in 1844 and ten years later took command of his first ship. The *Morgan* would be his second. He had married shortly before departing, and his wife Augusta was constantly on his mind during the voyage. He returned to find her mortally ill. After two years ashore he again commanded a whaleship, then remarried in Hawaii and finally settled in California. (MYSTIC SEAPORT MUSEUM, 1963.1500)

from a mobile population of men to work in an industry characterized by long voyages, boredom, personal antagonisms, and privation, interspersed with danger. Desertion actually worked to the benefit of whaleship owners as deserters had only the clothing advanced to them and the food served to them on board to compensate for their months of labor. Whaleships commonly called at Talcahuano, and the port had plenty of deserters from one ship looking for work on another, so Captain Hamilton easily replaced the deserters with a mix of American, English, Swedish, Portuguese, and South American men.

The captain had married only months before departing, and he filled his journal with longing for his wife, Augusta. From Talcahuano, he headed the ship north to whale but mostly to reach Lahaina, where Augusta's letters might await. After calling at Lahaina and Honolulu for supplies and to hire more men, the ship headed for the Sea of Okhotsk. In May, Hamilton toasted Augusta's birthday with a glass of champagne. By July, the ship was taking whales.

In August, the *Morgan* was one of seventeen American whaleships working in the Shantar Sea. When the ship's anchor fouled on something on the bottom, the ship *Harvest* sent over men to help, but they only succeeded in breaking the *Morgan*'s windlass. In the end they cut the cable and abandoned the anchor. Nevertheless, they had secured several whales and, on August 30, left the whaling grounds to return to Hawaii. Seven months later, the ship was headed back to the Sea of Okhotsk when, on April 7, 1861, Charles W. Morgan died at age sixty-four back in New Bedford.

The expanded hunt for right and bowhead whales, with their thick blubber, in icy seas had contributed to several innovations in the implements of whaling. First, back in 1848, the African American New Bedford shipsmith Lewis Temple had taken the principle of a Native Arctic toggle-headed spear to produce a harpoon with a pivoting head that would anchor itself when pulled upon. Temple did not patent his invention, so others copied it and made it easier to produce, but the concept remained his and boatsteerers found it much more reliable. The *Morgan* probably began to carry toggle harpoons in the 1850s. But even a toggle iron wasn't foolproof if the boatsteerer missed the whale when darting his iron. Captain Hamilton "broke"—demoted—two boatsteerers who missed.

In the early 1850s, Christopher Brand of Norwich, Connecticut, and several others developed cast-iron whaling guns to fire an explosive metal bomb into a whale to kill it. Bomb lance guns were especially useful in icy regions where a whale might escape under the ice before it could be lanced by hand. The extremely thick blubber of bowhead whales also made the hand lance far less reliable than a bomb lance as a killing tool. During this voyage, in June 1861, a bomb lance gun burst, wounding the hand of First Mate George Smith. As the ship's doctor, Captain Hamilton amputated a finger and dressed the hand, which healed successfully.

In 1865, Eben Pierce of New Bedford would patent a combination harpoon and lance. The toggle harpoon shaft with line attached was mounted on a pole fitted with a short barrel containing an exploding bomb. When the harpoon was darted, a rod fired the bomb lance into the whale, mortally wounding it, while the harpoon anchored the boat to the dying whale. Cheaper than a bomb lance gun, the Pierce or Pierce & Cunningham darting gun would be widely used in the later days of whaling.

Whaleboats also evolved from the 1830s to the 1870s. Early boats were generally built with overlapping planks fastened together through the edges (called lap-strake planking) while later boats commonly had smooth planking. The length of whaleboats for sperm whaling grew from about twenty-seven feet in 1840 to twenty-eight or twenty-nine feet by 1860, and those built for hunting right or bowhead whales in the Arctic might be thirty-one feet long. Whaleboat builders like the Beetle family of New Bedford also refined the whaleboat design for sailing, adding a hinged structure so the mast could be quickly stepped and lowered and installing a centerboard to make the boat more stable and to reduce leeway while sailing.

——◦◦◦◦◦◦——

As whaleships spent more time in cold climates, many were fitted with a "hurricane house" at the formerly exposed stern. To larboard, the hurricane house covered the officers' head (toilet) and the companionway (stairway) to the officers' quarters. To starboard, the house had a large storage locker, and in front of that was the ship's galley, with a larger and more sheltered and secure space for cooking than in the previous galley near the bow. The hurricane house also provided a roof over the wheel to shelter the helmsman and officer on deck. The *Morgan* was fitted with a hurricane house sometime between 1856 and the 1870s, possibly during the six-month layover in either 1859 or 1863.

——◦◦◦◦◦◦——

Refinement of whaleships included provisions for the lookouts who scanned the seas to sight the spouting of whales. When the *Morgan* first went to sea, the lookouts positioned themselves on an upper yard or clung to the royal (uppermost) section of mast. To make the task more efficient, whalemen devised a pair of iron hoops that were bolted to the mast above the royal crosstrees (supporting timbers). Lookouts could then stand on the crosstrees, with the hoops at chest level to give them a secure position. For whaling in cold seas, the hoops were sometimes shrouded with canvas to make a "crow's nest" mostly sheltered from the wind. The *Morgan* was equipped with hoops on the foremast and mainmast as the innovation spread through the fleet.

——◦◦◦◦◦◦——

In its worldwide expansion, the whaling industry benefited from, and contributed to, US government science. As superintendent of the US Navy's Depot of Charts and Instruments (later the Naval Observatory and Hydrographical Office), Navy Lieutenant Matthew Fontaine Maury started collecting data from ships' logbooks in about 1842. After analyzing the naval logs filed at the depot, he created a North

Atlantic wind and current chart in 1847. Captains who wished to obtain a chart had to agree to fill out and submit an abstract log, and Maury also had contributors abstract wind, current, and whale data from existing whaling and merchant-vessel logbooks, including those of the *Morgan*'s first two voyages. Maury also compiled logbook data on where different species of whales were encountered. By the 1850s, he had produced a whale chart of the oceans as well as additional wind and current charts that helped captains choose the most efficient routes across the seas. His work continued until he resigned from the US Navy to join the Confederacy in April 1861. With Maury's charts, even a relatively inexperienced captain like James Hamilton now had the resources to make the informed decisions that formerly had required many years of experience at sea.

<hr />

By October 1861, the *Charles W. Morgan* was headed back to Hawaii with 2,700 barrels of oil. At Honolulu in December 1861, Captain Hamilton discharged his first group of seasonal workers and signed on twenty men who also agreed to work for one year rather than the usual lay. Among them were the Samoans Charles, Frank, and John Perano. Henry Clay, Joe Carter, and Bob, Jack, Bill, and Friday Rotuman, were all natives of Rotuma, Fiji. Rotuma had been a popular stop for American whaleships since the 1820s, and island men frequently joined the crews. These six men had been deposited at Honolulu and were now willing to sign on board the *Morgan* for the term of one year, or one cruise, and then be returned to Honolulu. With the number of discharges, desertions, and seasonal hirings, more than one hundred men would fill the roughly thirty-five crew positions during this voyage.

Captain Hamilton then steered the ship in a new direction for a new form of whaling. Early New Englander shore whalers had depleted the Atlantic gray whale, which they called the scrag, by about 1700. In the North Pacific, a healthy population of gray whales bred and gave birth on the coast of Baja California in the winter and migrated north along the coast to Alaskan waters and back in the warm months. Their round trip of more than ten thousand miles is the longest of any animal's annual migration. California shore whalers had begun to take them as they passed in the 1850s, and in December 1857 Captain Charles M. Scammon had made a very successful voyage to the Baja lagoon, which became known as Scammon's Lagoon (now Laguna Ojo de Liebre), where they congregated.

Gray whales were smaller than right whales—growing to about forty-five feet in length and seventy thousand pounds—and had short baleen, but when they were plentiful the hunt was economical. By 1860, the whales were in decline, but the *Morgan* went after them nevertheless. At Scammon's Lagoon, ships would anchor and send their boats in to chase whales in the shallow lagoon, which was about five miles wide and two miles long, where the mother whales were nurturing their newborn before the migration north. They were so fierce in protecting their calves that some called them "devil fish." The *Morgan*'s boats crews found them "wild." One day, whales attacked and stove two boats and broke the thigh of one of the men in them. At the end of the challenging season, six men deserted and fled into the sand hills ashore.

The ship then returned to resupply at Hawaii and spend another season in the Sea of Okhotsk. On the way back to Honolulu, during an October gale, boatsteerer Ansel Braley fell overboard from aloft. The crew was able to launch a boat and rescue him, giving Captain Hamilton another medical challenge. Hamilton "found the mans jaw to be broken in two places, set it and bandaged it to the best of my ability. also bruised about the breast and one leg and side of his head. bad case. see out of neither eye. Bathed them with proper remidies. whilst lowering the boat mate got his arm and breast hurt some. tried to bleed him. Got no blood. Bathed the parts with sa[l]ve and sugar of lead &c . . . squalls dark and bad looking weather. so ends this day of casualties."

After paying off the seasonal men in Honolulu in December 1862, Captain Hamilton headed the ship for home. The *Morgan* continued to find and take whales during the slow passage, finally arriving at New Bedford on May 12, 1863. During the three years and seven months that the ship had been away, the nation had divided and was fighting a civil war. Defending slavery against the military, naval, and industrial strength of the North, the Confederate States commissioned commerce raiders to prey on US shipping. The most successful of these, the CSS *Alabama*, had raided off New England in the fall of 1862—while the *Morgan* was still in the Pacific—and off Brazil in the spring. Although the *Alabama* took twenty-nine US merchant vessels in the South Atlantic, the *Morgan* slipped by unawares.

War had also brought inflated prices and a scarcity of whale products. When the *Morgan* arrived, the whalebone (baleen) was worth $1.53 a pound, twice what it had been in 1859, and the value of whale oil had doubled as well. The cargo, worth $165,407.35 (about $3,983,000 today), was the largest in value, though not in quantity, that the ship ever brought in.

Sadly, despite the profit, Captain Hamilton arrived home to find Augusta to be terminally ill. After a marriage mostly spent in absentia, he would remain ashore for the next two years.

CHAPTER 5

Mrs. Landers Comes Aboard
1863–1867

Edward Mott Robinson had done very well with the *Charles W. Morgan* but, now in his sixties, he was ready to retrench his whaling business and move to New York. He would die there two years later. Robinson's assets would go to his daughter Hetty, who had assisted him in managing I. Howland Jr. & Company. In the year of her father's death she married shipping merchant Edward Green, and with him she had a son, Edward Howland Robinson Green, in 1868, and later a daughter. When her husband's business failed, Hetty Green settled into an extremely frugal style of living, as suited her Quaker upbringing, and invested her money shrewdly, becoming known as the "Queen of Wall Street," or sometimes the "Witch of Wall Street." When she died in 1916, she was probably the wealthiest woman in the world. Her son and daughter would enjoy the benefits, and Edward Howland Robinson Green would bring the *Charles W. Morgan* back into the Robinson family at a crucial time in the 1920s.

Edward Mott Robinson sold his 5/32 share in the *Morgan* to Joseph and William R. Wing, and they became her managing agent. Over the fifty-three years the *Morgan* remained in their management, they would increase their share to 35/64.

Unlike most whaleship agents, who had been captains or whale-oil producers, the Wings were clothing dealers who outfitted whalemen. Joseph Wing left his family's nearby farm to work in a New Bedford dry-goods store in 1833, and in 1849 he opened his own business. His younger brothers William and John became his partners, and they soon began to invest in whaleships. The Wings took over management of their first vessel in 1852, and by 1866 they would be agents for sixteen New Bedford whaleships. They profited from the clothing they sold their crews as well as from the sale of their oil and whalebone.

The Wings engaged Captain Thomas C. Landers of nearby Mattapoisett, who had recently returned from a Pacific whaling voyage, to take command of their new ship. Landers apparently took over Captain Hamilton's 1/32 share but later felt "cheated" that the Wings had not offered him a larger share in the ship. An entirely new crew, including the captain's thirteen-year-old son Arthur, came on

The J. & W. R. Wing house flag, with a blue W and a red ball in a blue field, flies from the main truck. The *Charles W. Morgan* flew this flag from 1863 to 1913. PHOTO BY ANDY PRICE. (MYSTIC SEA-PORT MUSEUM, D2014-06-0740)

board. While Second Mate William Harlow, a resident of Landers's hometown, and the third mate were in their late twenties, First Mate Charles W. Chace of Westport, Massachusetts, was just twenty-one.

The ship departed New Bedford on December 1, 1863, bound for the Cabo Verde Islands off northwest Africa. Fortunately, the CSS *Alabama* no longer threatened those waters, having sailed for the Indian Ocean to hunt US ships off Asia, and the new Confederate commerce raider *Florida* was blockaded in France.

The Portuguese had discovered the ten uninhabited Cabo Verde Islands in the 1400s and had used them as a depot in the slave trade. By the 1800s, the islands, especially Brava, the most fertile of the islands, also became important as a supply depot for American whaleships. When the *Morgan* called at Brava in January, the logbook recorded that they "took on board five hogs some Oranges three fowl and eight Portuguese." By this time, "Portuguese" crew members from Cabo Verde were of African Portuguese descent.

Captain Landers then set a course for Cape Horn and on to San Francisco. The captain was a widower who had recently married young Lydia Ann Goodspeed of Marston's Mills, Cape Cod. The couple agreed that she would accompany him

Captain Thomas C. Landers (1817–1877) of Falmouth, Massachusetts, was the first of the *Morgan*'s masters to take his wife to sea, installing a gimbaled (swinging) bed for her comfort. Despite the birth of a son during the voyage, the loss of his older son made the captain morose, and he argued frequently with his officers later in the voyage. He retired from whaling when the *Morgan* returned to New Bedford in 1867. (MYSTIC SEAPORT MUSEUM, 1973-4-77)

Lydia Ann Goodspeed Landers (1842–1921) of Cape Cod was twenty-one when she married Captain Landers two months before the *Morgan* departed. She joined the vessel at San Francisco and gave birth to a son at Guam in 1864, returning to the vessel when he was three weeks old. (MYSTIC SEAPORT MUSEUM, 1972-7-139)

during the voyage. Landers planned to spare her the passage round Cape Horn and had sent her by steamship and across the Isthmus of Panama to lodge at San Francisco's elegant Cliff House until the ship arrived.

As whaling voyages lengthened, an increasing number of captains had brought their wives and even children to sea since the 1840s. Despite the hardships, cramped quarters, and noxious business of cutting in and "boiling" oil, many women preferred to be with their husbands at sea rather than waiting at home alone for years. Some agents—including possibly the Wings—considered the presence of wives to be a distraction to the business of hunting whales. Others supported the idea. In 1849, Charles W. Morgan wrote, "this custom is becoming quite common and no disadvantages have been noticed. . . . There is more decency on board when there is a woman." Eventually, more than four hundred whaling captains' wives went to sea, making more than six hundred identified voyages.

To make Lydia Landers comfortable, her husband modified the captain's quarters. The narrow stateroom with its private head (water closet) remained on the starboard side, but the captain replaced the fixed fore-and-aft berth with a bedframe hanging on gimbals so that it would swing to remain level, no matter how much the ship heeled. This gimballed bed remains aboard today. Apparently, the captain also had the carpenter build a special gamming chair with rope slings so that Mrs. Landers could accompany him when visiting other whaleships at sea. The chair could be hoisted and lowered so that she did not have to climb the side of a ship.

On board, Lydia Landers lived a confined life. She likely ate breakfast, dinner, and supper at the mess table with her husband and the second and third mates (the first mate then being on duty on deck with his watch), served by the steward from his adjoining pantry. During the day, she might read or do needlework in the captain's day cabin with its upholstered sofa, a space about six feet by fifteen feet. If weather and work permitted, she might go on deck. There, she could walk or sit on the after deck. Traditionally, forward of the mainmast was the crew's portion of the deck and aft of the mainmast was the officers' area. Lydia Landers thus had an area extending about forty feet forward of the wheel and about twenty-two feet from rail to rail.

Captain Landers was following the ship's previous pattern of hunting sperm whales along the equator in winter and seeking bowheads in the Sea of Okhotsk in summer. While the *Morgan* was near Japan in June 1864, back in Washington, DC, President Abraham Lincoln signed a bill that established the Yosemite Grant to preserve that picturesque California valley for public use, which was the nation's first effort to conserve a portion of its natural environment.

On July 15, while tacking the ship on the way to the Shantar Sea, young Arthur Landers fell overboard. Before he could be rescued, he drowned. But there was no time to concentrate on grief, and whaling continued routinely through the summer.

When it became evident that Lydia Landers was pregnant, the captain headed for the island of Guam, where she could give birth. The couple named their baby Arthur in honor of his dead half-brother. When he was three weeks old, Mrs. Landers brought him aboard and the voyage continued. However, the death of his first son may have eaten at the captain, as Mate Chace noted his short temper in several entries in the ship's logbook. At one point, in the presence of Mrs. Landers, the captain found fault with the coffee and pulled the steward out of his pantry and kicked him on deck. Eventually, one of the mates asked, "what is the matter here Capt, you are always in a row."

Although the Civil War was nearly over when the *Morgan* approached the Sea of Okhotsk in the spring of 1865, the CSS *Shenandoah* had not received the news and was headed for the same area, hunting for defenseless whaleships. The *Shenandoah* burned one whaler in May before a barrier of ice prevented access to the Sea of Okhotsk. Changing course, the commerce raider headed north for the Bering Strait, where it destroyed two dozen whaleships in late June. If not for the ice, the *Morgan* might have become a victim of the Civil War, though its destruction would have come after the war had ended.

After a successful season in 1865, the ship returned to Hawaii. That winter the *Morgan* made another pass through the Caroline Islands, north of Papua New Guinea and south of Guam, before heading for the Sea of Japan on the way to the Sea of Okhotsk. Landers and Mate Chace had a set-to that season when the captain gave Chace a vague order and then countermanded what Chace did. After a flurry of curses and name-calling, Landers relieved the mate of duty and sent him to his stateroom but soon reinstated him. Later, when young Bartholomew Sullivan's boat failed to take a whale, the captain ordered the ship to sail off. After Sullivan's boat finally overtook the ship, Sullivan confronted the captain. When another mate and part of the crew backed Sullivan, Landers had one man confined in irons (handcuffs), at which point part of the crew nearly mutinied.

Discipline on board broke down after this. Men were found drunk on duty, and some men were confined in double irons. Men deserted in the islands, and two recruits from the Mariana Islands north of Guam fell from aloft; one of them died. Then the contention between Landers and Chace arose again, bringing them almost to a fist fight.

That fall, the ship called at Tahiti before heading for Cape Horn. Lydia Landers and two-year-old Arthur remained on board for the eastbound passage. Coming up the Atlantic, the ship stopped at Barbados in the West Indies. There, six of the crew stole a boat and deserted. The steward, who had been held in irons for several weeks, went ashore to lodge a complaint against the captain with the American consul there but deserted instead.

The *Morgan* arrived back in New Bedford on June 12, 1867. The wartime boom in whale products was long over by then. The Wings sold the cargo for $58,125 (about $1,198,500 in 2023), which they calculated worked out to $45.19 per day for the 1,286-day voyage.

For his part, Captain Landers retired with Lydia to his home in Mattapoisett and remained ashore. They would have three more children on dry land before his death in 1877.

From Ship to Bark
1867-1881

The *Charles W. Morgan* that left New Bedford on July 17, 1867, bore little resemblance to the ship that had sailed in 1841. In the month since it had arrived, the Wings had employed riggers who removed the square yards from the mizzen mast and converted the ship into a bark. With only a fore-and-aft spanker and triangular topsail now on that mast, the ship's rigging was reduced by about one quarter. However, the changes made the vessel more maneuverable in sailing to windward and negotiating confined waters, such as in the Sea of Okhotsk. The ship also received a new protective layer of copper sheets on the bottom.

At this time the Wings also upgraded the ship from a four-boat to a five-boat whaler, adding a larboard bow boat, a fourth mate to command it, and at least five additional crew members. Also in 1867, government tonnage rules for measuring vessels were changed, and the *Morgan*'s registered tonnage (though not her actual dimensions or volume) was reduced from 351 to 313.75.

For captain, the Wings engaged George Athearn, who had left the family farm at West Tisbury on Martha's Vineyard to go to sea as a boy and had later commanded the *Emily Morgan*. Alvin H. Davis returned to the ship as first mate, and the captain's relative, twenty-nine-year-old Edwin Athearn, came on board as fourth mate. Two men deserted just before the vessel departed.

The ship first headed east to the Azores for supplies and additional crew members. Captain Athearn then spent a month hunting whales around the Azores while making repairs and alterations to the new bark rig. Several men had already had enough and deserted at Faial in early September. Whales remained scarce until the ship was in the South Atlantic. On October 4, John Frates sighted "a shoal of sperm whales going to the windward," for which he would receive a $50 bounty. The larboard, waist, and bow boats all struck and killed their whales, though the waist boat overturned during the action.

On October 29, the *Morgan* encountered the New Bedford whaleship *Henry Taber* off the Rio de la Plate, and the two vessels gammed for several days. The *Morgan* was now in one of the principal regions for feeding and breeding among humpback whales. As humpbacks were fast and did not produce much oil for the effort of killing them, American whalemen seldom hunted that species. But, on November 11, Mate Davis recorded: "two Hump Backs come clost to Ship I shot a Bom

Lance in one hurt him pretty bad lowrd 2 Boats I shot him again & brok my Nose gun kicked very bad." As it was late, they did not secure the injured humpback.

Continuing south, the *Morgan* rounded Cape Horn on November 27 and headed up the coast of Chile in search of whales. Other ships were taking whales there, and finally on February 10 the larboard boat struck a whale; however, after about five hours, it was "cut from the Whale & came a board Whale spouting good Blood could not hall to him to Lance." On February 13, Third Mate Bodine sighted whales at 6 a.m. At 7:30 a.m., they lowered three boats, the waist boat struck, and, by 11 a.m., they had the whale alongside to be cut in.

At the beginning of March 1868, the ship called at San Carlos, Chile, to take on water, firewood, and potatoes. Each day one of the watches was given liberty on shore, and each day a man deserted, with four running on March 12, including John Frates who had gotten the bounty for sighting whales.

After more whaling off Chile, the *Morgan* worked up to the Galápagos Islands where it had some success before heading west along the line (equator). By late June they were in the Marquesas (which Herman Melville had described in his 1846 book *Typee: A Peep at Polynesian Life*). Captain Athearn went ashore on Fatu Hiva

(Magdelena to the whalemen) to obtain supplies, bringing aboard twenty-three hogs, three hundred coconuts, and bananas. In mid-July they headed to Tahiti "to procure medical ade for the Captain he having a bad sore on his Ankle." The *Morgan* lay there for three weeks while the captain received care ashore. During the interlude, Mate Davis overhauled the rigging and shipped a couple of new men, while six men deserted. Once Captain Athearn came aboard and the *Morgan* departed, they discovered "3 more Kanakas stowd away"—John Orrotanga, Jim Mangra, and Bob Whytootak—who promptly became crew members.

At Tahiti, boatsteerer John E. D. Smith joined the crew. At various times he gave his place of birth as New York State and "at sea" in the English Channel, but he would make his home aboard the *Charles W. Morgan*. For the next twenty-three years he would make seven voyages in the *Morgan*, missing only the 1887–1888 and 1888–1889 voyages, before he retired from the sea at nearly age sixty in 1891. Serving first as boatsteerer and later as carpenter, cooper, and shipkeeper, Smith would put in more time and more miles aboard the *Morgan* than any other individual.

The *Morgan* continued to whale without success along the line and in September returned to Tahiti. With so much desertion among this crew, Athearn and Davis cracked down. When four of the previous deserters were sent out to the vessel, "I put them in Irons & putt them in the Blubber Room," recorded Mate Davis. When two more were sent on board on September 7, he recorded, "I putt them in Irons & put them down in the Fore Hole." After the captain returned on September 10, Davis "putt all the runways in the riggin. Joseph Barre Jules Nicklas give 1 dozen [lashes] each[,] took the other 4 out of the Irons going to keep them on Deck 4 months no watch below day time[,] putt Joseph Barre & Jules Nicklas in Irons & put them in the Fore Hole so ends." Barre and Nicholas were Azoreans who had been aboard since the beginning of the voyage. A few days later they were returned to work.

Captain Athearn then headed for the New Zealand grounds in search of right whales. Although they found the whales "wild," on October 23 former deserter Jules Nicholas sighted a whale and they lowered all four boats. "Capt struck took his line Bow Boat struck the whale & I killd him." Right whales were abundant, and on October 31 Captain Athearn sighted another. Three boats were lowered, recorded Mate Davis, "I wnet on & Boat steer mist At 2 P.M. came a board at 2 1/2 P.M. loard a gain for a nother I went on & struck at 5 P.M. had him a long side and all ready for cutting at 10 had him cut in."

By the end of 1869 the *Morgan* was back off the coast of Chile, hunting sperm whales. On April 1, 1870, just after noon, they sighted a burning ship in the distance and "made all sail & steerd for him." It was the ship *Sunbeam* of Boston, bound home from Iquique, Chile, with a cargo of saltpeter. When varnish vapors ignited, the ship exploded in flames and sank in twenty minutes with the loss of six men. The *Morgan* arrived to save thirteen survivors in the ship's boat and take them in to Talcahuano.

There, Captain Athearn gave the men liberty while resupplying the ship with fresh water, bread, and flour. Another four men deserted there, and the captain found five replacements.

Still whaling on the Chilean coast, the Morgan approached a derelict bark on October 2. It was the Italian bark *Cincinatte* of Genoa, loaded with Peruvian guano (bird dung), which was in worldwide demand for fertilizer. The bark was abandoned, so Captain Athearn salvaged some sails, rigging, and cabin provisions before the vessel sank.

Having a respectable cargo of sperm and right-whale oil on board, Captain Athearn decided to head for the Atlantic in December 1870. The ship rounded Cape Horn on December 29 and called at the Falkland Islands as she worked her way north.

On Wednesday, January 25, 1871, a new hand wrote in the logbook: "At 6 3/4 Mr. Davis the mate was taken very sudden with heart disease he died immediately and never spoke a word at 8 p.m. laid him out middle part blowing fresh. . . . employed making a coffin." The next day, "latter part the same with foggy weather got the coffin up and put it under the boat on the house set the course, jib, and spanker so ends." Having begun his whaling career on board the *Charles W. Morgan* eighteen years earlier, Alvin H. Davis ended his life on the same vessel.

Promoted from second to first mate, Frederick Swain continued the succinct recording of the daily details of the vessel's business in the logbook. Death of a shipmate, no matter how close, was recorded without emotion, and the daily routines of ship-handling continued.

The *Morgan* spent February and March whaling off the Rio de la Plate, where it took several sperm whales. The vessel then headed for Barbados, arriving in April. There, four men deserted and two joined the crew. From Barbados the *Morgan* headed for the "Western Ground" near Bermuda, where the crew found more sperm whales. After three months of cruising there, the vessel was "bound home."

On August 14, they "bundled the boats craft [harpoons and lances] and hove the tryworks overboard." This informal ceremony confirmed the end of the voyage. It was also a necessary step as the brick tryworks was built over a water-filled box called the goose pen, which insulated the deck from the heat of the tryworks fires. Removing the tryworks allowed the deck to dry. The two large pots themselves were kept on board, but the worn bricks were discarded.

The *Charles W. Morgan* arrived back in New Bedford on August 16, 1871. The Wings would sell the oil and bone for $54,975 (about $1,280,367 in 2023) and calculated that the vessel had produced an average of $36.27 a day during the 1,491-day voyage.

The Wings took about six weeks to refit the *Charles W. Morgan* and have a new tryworks built. While the vessel lay safe in port, forty other American whaling vessels were in the Arctic Sea, working along the north coast of Alaska in search of bowheads. This branch of the industry brought more vessels farther into the icy Arctic

On the New Bedford waterfront in about 1870, William R. Wing (center) poses with his daughters Clara and Helen and shipkeeper Frank Lewis. Casks of whale oil rest in the background, waiting for processing, while the whaling bark *Massachusetts* has its sails set for drying. (MYSTIC SEAPORT MUSEUM, 1994.53.34)

each year. This year, the wind and ice shifted at the beginning of September, trapping and crushing thirty-three vessels, twenty-two of which were from New Bedford. Ariel Norton, second mate during the *Morgan*'s 1853 voyage, was in command of the *Awashonks* when it was crushed, and he was one of the 1,219 who escaped by boat and were carried to Honolulu by the seven vessels that escaped the ice. The *Morgan* would never enter the Arctic Ocean.

On September 26, 1871, the *Charles W. Morgan* left New Bedford under the command of thirty-two-year-old John M. Tinkham of Mattapoisett. Headed for the Azores, the crew sighted a whale just two weeks out on October 6. Although the starboard boat fastened but was stove, with two men hurt, the larboard and bow boats secured the whale. Ten days later they got another sperm whale, though the captain's boat got "rolled over" in the process.

After a typical stop in Faial, the *Morgan* headed south to Tristan da Cunha for supplies. During a short cruise in those waters, the crew took a whale. From there, Captain Tinkham set a course around the Cape of Good Hope and into the Indian Ocean. First they headed to the Crozet Islands, 1,500 miles southeast of the Cape in the south Indian Ocean, seeking right whales. These six islands had been discovered in 1772, and by the early 1800s had become a destination for sealers. After 1835, whalers began to frequent the region. In *Moby-Dick*, Herman Melville referred to the Crozets as "a good cruising ground for Right Whalemen." Even in the southern hemisphere summer, the seas were turbulent, and, on January 23, 1872, Theodore Bennet fell from the main yard. As the *Morgan* sailed by, they threw him a line and began to lower a boat, but it was too late to save him. A month later, on February 23, they took three sperm whales and took four more on April 8 and 10.

By late July, they were in Antongil Bay on the northeast coast of the island of Madagascar, east of Africa. With the decline of sperm- and right-whale stocks on the customary grounds, whalemen were in search of alternatives. They had generally avoided humpbacks because of their speed and their relatively lean blubber. Although they are baleen whales, humpbacks, with their long pectoral fins, are rorquals (with lined, greatly expandable skin below their lower jaws), related more closely to blue and finback whales than to right whales or bowheads. Different humpback populations inhabit specific ocean regions. One group gathered to breed and feed in Antongil Bay.

When the *Morgan* took two humpbacks, they produced only about forty-five barrels of oil. The vessel would spend months cruising over the seven hundred miles between Madagascar and Mauritius and stopping at Réunion Island, four hundred miles east of Madagascar. On November 28, "about 1 P.M. Starboard boat struck stove and parted line. Capt. Tinkham received quite a severe blow on his head cutting it." Steward Hiram Look recorded his observations from the voyage: "the Bom gun is used mostly where the Whale Is desperate. Oh a desperate Whale is a Relular tirant." Look remarked, "Sperm Whales fight with their emence great mouth and like the Right whale with their emence tail." If the boat avoided the whale's fury and succeeded in harpooning and lancing, with the whale "spouting thick blood," the mate "orders the Boat Steerer to slack line away from the whale. Then we knew the whale is Dieing. *Its termed going into the Flury.*" Look added a myth of whalemen: "They roll around showing great agony and raise their head out of water, roll on Their Left side with their Head pointing East and all is over."

<hr />

In a land analogy to the decline of whale stocks, in 1870 about ten million bison roamed the Great Plains, where the Cheyenne, Comanche, and Siouxan groups, who had developed a horse culture in the 1700s, revered them, hunted them for food, and made use of their hides, sinews, and other parts. But, after the Civil War, homesteaders were moving onto the plains to settle and farm, railroads were

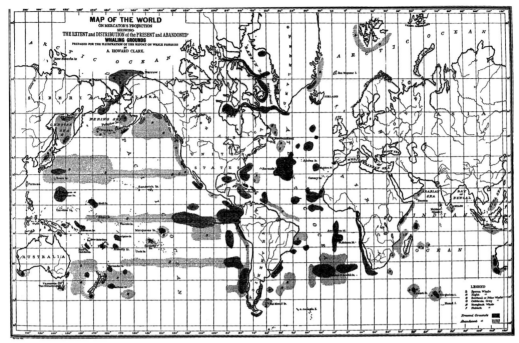

The world's whaling grounds were detailed in this map from an 1887 map from a US government report. (MYSTIC SEAPORT MUSEUM, 1991-6-263)

extending west and trying to keep their tracks free of obstacles, and the US government began to restrict the free movement and hunting of the Native peoples and to confine them to reservations. Beginning in 1871, bison hunters began to slaughter the herds, killing 5,000 a day and 3,650,000 annually in 1871 and '72. Some of the hides were shipped to Germany, where the leather could be processed, the tongues might be saved for food, but most of the carcasses were left where they lay and were later scavenged for the bones. By 1889, only an estimated eighty-five bison roamed free (with one thousand others in protected herds and zoos).

But, even as this slaughter had intensified, in March 1872, while the *Morgan* pursued whales off Madagascar, the US Congress established Yellowstone National Park, the world's first national park, which protected a herd of two hundred bison. The nation had begun to see more than simple profit in the natural world.

In 1874, Captain Charles Melville Scammon, who had begun the hunt for gray whales nineteen years earlier and since 1863 had served in the US Revenue Cutter Service, published his study, *The Marine Mammals of the North-western Coast of North America*. Fascinated by the creatures he hunted, he had collected specimens and looked deeply into their natural history. This book combined his physical and behavioral description of a variety of animals, from whales to walruses, with a history of whaling in the North Pacific to that time. Although Scammon's book did not sell well, it is still considered the first serious study of an ocean's marine mammals.

Scammon's appreciation of their physical and social complexity was quite a contrast to the prevailing view of them as simple commercial products to be harvested.

—◦◦◦◦◦—

During the *Morgan*'s hunt in the Indian Ocean, Steward Hiram Look considered Captain Tinkham "a brutal and most contemptable Man. Meanness does not name it. He was an Ignoramus of the First Quality." Look was happy to return to New Bedford on October 31, 1874, after three years and one month. The oil and whalebone were valued at $69,060 (about $1,848,000 in 2023), which averaged out to a good $64.27 per day for the 1,132 days at sea. Hiram Look had arranged for his mother and sister to receive advances on his lay, which left him just $57.21 (about $1,530 in 2023) as his share. Third Mate Frank Roderick earned an additional $60 as a bounty for sighting six whales during the voyage.

The Wings then refitted the *Morgan*. The hull was stripped, recaulked, and recoppered. The bulwarks (rails) were rebuilt, and the bitts that stabilized the bowsprit were replaced. Sparmakers shaped several new yards and mast sections, and riggers installed some new wire rigging, which was stronger and thinner than the old, thick hemp stays.

The renewed vessel was ready for sea in April 1875. After his successful voyage, Captain Tinkham was back in command. Two days after his return in October, he had married twenty-year-old Clara Taber, and she would accompany him on this voyage. Captain Tinkham had a small deck house built for her, so she could find shelter on deck. She was musical, so she brought a small organ to sea. With her sitting room on deck and the sound of parlor music below, she would seemingly make more of an impression on the vessel than Lydia Landers had.

As before, the *Morgan* spent time whaling off the Azores and in the South Atlantic. At the southwest end of her cruises was the island of St. Helena. Discovered by Portuguese mariners in the early 1500s, St. Helena had been taken as a British East India Company supply point in the 1600s. After the Napoleonic Wars, Napoleon Bonaparte was exiled there between 1815 and his death in 1821. Thereafter, as a Crown colony, the island was visited by a thousand ships a year, calling there for fresh water or supplies.

Again during this voyage, desertions became frequent. At the Cabo Verde islands in November 1875, sixteen men ran from the vessel and were replaced by islanders. At Faial, Azores, in June 1876, six of those men were among the thirteen who deserted. Possibly reflecting Captain Tinkham's difficult personality, sixty-six men would serve on board during the three-year voyage, and only seven men stayed on board with Tinkham for the entire trip.

Clara Tinkham had an uncomfortable adjustment to whaling life. She later told a newspaper reporter, "The smell of blubber, pigs and hens running about the deck and having to eat food made of sour dough are just a few of the things that make the life offensive to a woman." She also suffered from seasickness, and after a year and a half she left the ship at St. Helena in November 1876. She took a steamship to England and another to America, where she returned home to await her husband.

The *Morgan* continued to cruise in the South Atlantic between St. Helena and the African coast, several times calling at the bay of Cabinda, just north of the mouth of the Congo River. When the vessel arrived back at New Bedford on May 17, 1878, it landed a small cargo worth just $31,869 (about $972,300 in 2023)—a $28.21 return per day for the 1,119-day voyage. With a 1/60th lay worth $526, carpenter John E. D. Smith received just $47.90 (about $1,460 in 2023) after the deductions for his advance and his expenses at sea. Captain Tinkham took his lay and retired with Clara to a farm in Mattapoisett.

———◦∞◇∞◦———

The shipfitters got to work once more. Caulkers resealed the *Morgan*'s topsides, and new copper was applied to the bottom. Sparmakers were busy turning a new foremast, mainmast, and bowsprit, all of which were three feet shorter than the originals. They also produced a new main topsail yard and main topgallant mast. Parts of the rigging were also replaced.

After just two months, the *Morgan* was ready for sea. A new captain, Thomas L. Ellis, thirty, and a new crew came on board, along with the vessel's fixture, carpenter John E. D. Smith. Ellis was a native of Dartmouth, upriver from New Bedford, and had gone to sea aboard the bark *James Arnold* at age fourteen in 1862. Captain Ellis followed Captain Tinkham's pattern in whaling off the Azores, Cabo Verdes, St. Helena, and Cabinda in the South Atlantic. The vessel returned to New Bedford on May 11, 1881, with a cargo worth $47,588.59 (about $1,423,375 in 2023), which the Wings figured to be $46.29 a day during the 1,028-day voyage. Cook John Harding, a thirty-nine-year-old Black man from Nova Scotia, had signed aboard for a 1/145th lay plus half the value of the "slush," or grease, that he collected from cooking during the voyage. His lay was worth $328.19, and his half of the slush was worth $18.00, but his advance and expenses during the voyage, with interest, added up to $389.10. After 1,000 days at sea, he owed the Wings $42.91 (about $1,283 in 2023).

CHAPTER 7

The Longest Voyage
1881-1886

As the Wings prepared the *Morgan* to return to sea, most likely the vessel was "hove down," with heavy block and tackle anchored to the wharf, pulling against the lower masts to roll the hull down and expose half the bottom at a time. Then the bottom was scraped and recaulked, and new copper sheathing was applied. During the operation, an eight-inch-thick timber called the shoe was spiked to the bottom of the keel, adding to the vessel's steerageway and serving as protection to the keel itself.

Shipwrights came aboard to refasten the ceiling (inner planking) in the lower hold and to check the copper fastenings of the planks. After forty years—about twice the serviceable life of wooden merchant ships—the *Morgan* would be strong and tight.

On deck, the windlass was moved. Originally, this large, horizontal structure was located aft of the foremast and may have been operated by the sheer strength of the crew turning it with handspikes. But, in this refit, the windlass was moved forward of the mast and just aft of the small foredeck on which the anchors were stowed. Rather than handspikes, the new windlass was operated by a pump-break mechanism, with long levers to crank a ratchet system, reducing the labor of the crew. During this operation, the forecastle companionway was displaced by the windlass and moved aft of the foremast. Before a new tryworks was built, the coamings for the fore hatch, through which many barrels had been raised and lowered, were rebuilt.

The bowsprit was also replaced, as were some shrouds and stays, now in wire rope rather than hemp. Aloft, the vessel received a new configuration on its mainmast. The lower yard was replaced, and the large topsail was replaced by modern double topsails. As merchant ships had grown in size since 1850, the big, deep topsails became difficult to manage and to reef in heavy winds. In the 1850s, several innovators found ways to divide the topsail in half, adding an extra yard to make two smaller sails. The lower one, on a fixed yard, would become the principal heavy-weather square sail. The upper topsail yard could be raised to set the sail and lowered to furl the sail. The *Morgan* was rather late in having this conversion made. During the voyage, carpenter John E. D. Smith would shape an upper topmast yard for the foremast, and then the vessel would be fully up to date. For long-distance

The *Charles W. Morgan* stands aback while retrieving a whaleboat. PHOTO BY DENNIS A. MURPHY.
(MYSTIC SEAPORT MUSEUM, D2014-07-1064)

sailing, the *Morgan* still carried royals (the square sail above the topgallant), but these were commonly sent down while cruising on the whaling grounds.

Captain Charles F. Keith, forty-eight, of Fairhaven, who had gone to sea at sixteen and first commanded the Mattapoisett whaling bark *Annawan* in 1857, came aboard for this voyage. Joseph King, a forty-nine-year-old from Cabo Verde, returned as second mate, and John Harding was back as cook. Third Mate Peter John, thirty-two, was also from Cabo Verde, while Fourth Mate James Howland, twenty-three, came from Rochester, Massachusetts, inland from New Bedford. Captain Keith's brother William also joined the crew.

The *Morgan* departed New Bedford on July 13, 1881, bound for the Azores as usual. The voyage began well, with sperm whales sighted nine times in 1881. The crew took three, and one of them produced 140 barrels. As the vessel worked south toward Cabo Verde on November 17, at 4:20 in the morning, Fourth Mate Howland ran below to report a fire in the fore hold. It was extinguished before it blazed up, but it was apparent that someone had soaked oakum in kerosene and set it afire. Jose and Lawrence Correa reported seeing Harry Wilson, twenty-two, and William Morey, seventeen, opening the fore hatch, and Jose saw them light the fire. Steward George Yale was also implicated, and all three were placed in irons. After the *Morgan* reached Brava, Cabo Verde, Wilson and Morey would desert in early December.

At Brava on November 30, the *Morgan* was moving slowly as Fourth Mate Howland and William Keith began lowering the starboard boat. When the after davit broke, both men were plunged into the water. The men on deck threw them an oar. Keith could swim, but Howland drowned before Keith could save him. From Cabo Verde, the *Morgan* continued south, following the recent pattern of rounding the Cape of Good Hope into the Indian Ocean and heading for the stormy Crozets. There the vessel was further damaged when a davit broke and the waist boat was lost.

On May 28, 1882, the *Morgan* reached Mangonui on Doubtless Bay in northeast New Zealand. Similar to the Bay of Islands, this was a convenient supply point for cruising in search of right and sperm whales. For the rest of 1882 and 1883, the vessel cruised the waters around Chatham Island, Pitt Island (Rangiauria), and French Rock, east of New Zealand. In 1882, they sighted sperm whales eight times, taking four, and right whales eleven times, taking seven. In 1883, they sighted sperm whales eight times, taking three, and right whales nine times, taking three. In July 1883, carpenter Smith finished shaping the fore upper topmast yard, completing the conversion of the rig to double topsails.

That fall, a succession of gales kept the vessel riding out the wind and waves with the barest of sails set. Foremast hand Earl Russell, seventeen, somehow contracted typhoid and was buried at sea on November 28. Captain Keith then came down with a fever, and, on January 31, 1884, he went ashore on remote, sparsely settled Pitt Island to recuperate. At some point, Mrs. Keith and their young son had joined the ship. It is possible they had been aboard since the beginning, but more likely they had traveled out by ship and joined the *Morgan* in New Zealand. They are not mentioned in the logbook until they went ashore with Captain Keith, and they remained on Pitt Island when he returned to the *Morgan* on February 7. They would rejoin the *Morgan* in July, but it appears that Mrs. Keith may have had enough and would return to New Zealand to find a ship home. Steward George Yale had deserted at Mangonui in 1884 and was replaced by Scotsman Robert Craig, who had joined the vessel in 1883. On April 12, 1885, he died of Bright's disease—nephritis, or kidney inflammation—and was buried at sea the next day.

Two frustrating years of gales, few whales, and many desertions continued through 1884 and 1885. In 1884, they sighted sperm whales just four times and took none. Right whales appeared six times. They took two but lost one of them when the fluke chain broke before they could cut in the whale. From the whales taken, they tried out 8,915 gallons of right-whale oil and extracted, cleaned, and dried 7,618 pounds of baleen, which Captain Keith shipped home from New Zealand. They would see no more right whales. In 1885 they sighted sperm whales seven times but were unable to take any of them, and in 1886 they sighted them five times but would take only one.

On March 1, 1886, Captain Keith set a course for Cape Horn, bound home at last. While the vessel would ride the prevailing winds across the Pacific rather than fight them in the Indian Ocean, all did not go well. Sailing before the wind under foresail and lower topsails on March 24, the *Morgan* was overtaken by a monstrous wave that broke over her stern, smashing into the house, washing away the wheel, and flooding the deck. The crew hove to under bare poles and rode with the sea while repairs were made. By the next day, they had reconstructed the wheel and the vessel squared away under topsails toward Cape Horn.

The *Morgan* rounded Cape Horn on April 2 and passed Bermuda on June 8. On June 14, with the voyage considered over, the crew dismantled the tryworks and threw the bricks overboard, and they unrigged the cutting tackle. For a voyage that turned up few whales, it was ironic that the crew raised a sperm whale the next day. Captain Keith ordered the boats lowered, and they secured the whale. The crew then rehung the cutting tackles so they could cut in the whale. Without tryworks, they resorted to the old method of cutting up the blubber and stowing it in casks to be tried out ashore.

On June 18, 1886, the *Morgan* entered New Bedford Harbor. During the entire voyage, they had sighted sperm whales thirty-six times, taking eleven of them, which produced 850 barrels of oil. They saw right whales twenty-six times, taking thirteen but losing two. When the cargo was unloaded and assessed, it was valued at $46,693.34 (about $1,515,600 in 2023), but it had taken 1,801 days—a month less than five years—to get it. In the Wings' computations, that worked out to just $25.17 per day. This was the *Morgan*'s longest and least profitable (when calculated by day) voyage.

CHAPTER 8

Outward Bound from San Francisco

1886-1890

After the long absence and hard usage, the *Morgan* was ready for another refit. The Wings had shipwrights check the hull over thoroughly, add some knees to reinforce the deck beams, refasten the planks where needed, and rebuild much of the stern after the damage suffered at sea. To make the vessel more efficient, they added a small "steeple" (vertically aligned) compound steam donkey engine. The design, with both high-pressure and low-pressure pistons on the same shaft, made a small engine quite powerful and needed less space than a horizontal engine. It would drive a belt that, through gearing, would operate the

Furling the main course. PHOTO BY ANDY PRICE. (MYSTIC SEAPORT MUSEUM, D2014-06-103)

J. & W. R. Wing advertised their New Bedford clothing store in the whalemen's newspaper, the *Whalemen's Shipping List and Merchants' Transcript*, through the 1880s. The Wings profited from both selling clothing to their whalemen (with interest charged during the voyage) and selling the whale products their crews delivered. (MYSTIC SEAPORT MUSEUM, 1993-3-9)

windlass when raising anchor or cutting in a whale. The engine and its small boiler were apparently installed in the blubber room, just aft of the forecastle on the larboard side, with a smoke pipe rising near the rail by the larboard shrouds. Merchant ships had begun to carry steam donkey engines for raising anchors and sails in the 1870s to reduce the size of the crew (although a steam engine required a skilled engineer to operate it). Since a whaleship's crew size was set by the number of whaleboats it carried, the *Morgan*'s engine was more for efficiency. The engine cost $1,225.

The Wings also had the *Morgan*'s bow reinforced with heavy timbers. For almost twenty years they had been sending the *Morgan* to relatively temperate seas in the Atlantic, Pacific, and Indian Oceans, searching for sperm and right whales. Meanwhile, much of the whaling fleet was turning to Arctic whaling for bowheads, despite the dangers there, represented by the many vessels lost to the ice in 1871. At the same time, San Francisco had grown into one of the principal Pacific ports, with connections to the East Coast via the transcontinental railroad and steamship lines connecting the coasts via the railroad across Panama. To save the many months of transit between New Bedford and the North Pacific, whaling firms began to base their operations in San Francisco. With ice now setting the schedule for access to whales, the vessels began to make one-year voyages out of San Francisco, whaling in the open sea in spring, venturing north as summer arrived, then returning to San Francisco to deliver their cargo and refit in the fall (although a few steam whalers were built to overwinter in the Arctic, spending several whaling seasons there before returning to San Francisco). The establishment of the large Arctic Oil Works at San Francisco in 1883 provided a new West-Coast production facility for the oil and baleen, confirming San Francisco's new importance as a whaling port.

The Wings would now send their vessels *Charles W. Morgan*, *Alice Knowles*, and *Cape Horn Pigeon* to San Francisco to take up this routine. Each year, William R. Wing would travel from New Bedford to San Francisco in the late fall, when the vessels returned and refitted for their next voyage, to manage their accounts.

The Wings selected Captain George A. Smith to command the *Morgan*. A native of Eastport, Maine, Smith had transplanted himself to New Bedford and gone whaling as a young man. He was first mate for the *Morgan*'s profitable 1859–1863 voyage, when he lost a finger to a bomb-lance gun. After serving as a naval officer during the Civil War, he returned to whaling, rising to command in 1869. Now he was back aboard the *Morgan*, almost thirty years later, as master.

While John E. D. Smith, now fifty-three, returned as carpenter, the rest of the crew members were new and of widely varied origins. First Mate John S. Layton had just returned from four years as mate on the whaling bark *Sunbeam*. Born at Freemantle, Australia, in 1845, Layton was an American whaleman by 1871. Boat-steerer Honorio P. Martin, a thirty-four-year-old native of Brava, was one of two boatsteerers and five seamen from Cabo Verde. James Antone, George Brown, and William McKutchinson were Black men from the West Indies, and Crispolo de Aris and Marcellino Rose were from the Philippines. Joseph Bement, twenty-two, was a greenhand from New York.

With help from the new steam engine, the crew raised the anchor on October 6, 1886. The voyage started turbulently. Two men deserted just before the vessel left New Bedford. At sea, Joseph Bement was hazed and ridiculed by others in the crew for his sullen behavior. When he attacked Mate Layton, Bement was wrestled into submission and flogged.

Bement remembered Captain Smith as short-tempered and prone to outbursts. "You knew he was mad when he started to stutter," remarked Bement. "The mad-der he got the more he stuttered." Bement recalled the crew referring to their captain—in private—as "Stuttering George."

The *Morgan* followed a familiar route through the South Atlantic, past the Cape of Good Hope, and across the Indian Ocean. By the end of February 1887, the vessel had arrived at Norfolk Island, between Australia and New Zealand, a former penal settlement where the descendants of the HMS *Bounty* mutineers had been relocated from Pitcairn Island in 1856. The *Morgan* then headed north, anchoring at Guam in the Northern Mariana Islands in early April to resupply. This island, colonized by Spain in 1565, lies 1,500 miles southeast of Japan. The native Chamorro population of Guam had dwindled and intermarried with Spanish, Japanese, and Caroline Islanders. Guam had been a port of call for whaleships working the Japan grounds since 1823, and young men of Guam became willing recruits to go whaling.

At Guam, Joseph Bement went ashore with a boat's crew to obtain water and fresh fruit for the crew. Once ashore, he and three others ran, concealing themselves in the hills among the thick undergrowth. They were still on the loose five days later when Captain Smith signed on four new hands, offering them smaller lays than those of the fugitives they were

Captain George A. Smith (1828–1891) had first sailed on the *Morgan* as mate for the 1859–1863 voyage. He returned to command the vessel for the 1886–1887 voyage to San Francisco and the 1887–1888 voyage out of San Francisco. (COURTESY OF THE MARTHA'S VINEYARD MUSEUM)

replacing. Bement would serve on trading vessels in the Pacific before returning to New York. The scars of his flogging remained on his back for the rest of his life. A hundred years after his time on the *Morgan*, his family donated to Mystic Seaport Museum a set of "bones"—a simple percussion instrument favored by sailors—that he had carried.

On April 14, 1887, the *Morgan* left Guam and headed for the Sea of Okhotsk. After a summer on the grounds it had frequented during the 1863 voyage with Captain Smith as mate, the vessel headed east across the North Pacific, entering San Francisco Bay for the first time on November 4, 1887. After a year and one month at sea, the *Morgan* delivered a cargo worth $33,646 (about $1,083,000 in 2023).

───◦◦◇◦◦───

It was only a year since the vessel had been overhauled in New Bedford, so it took little time to outfit it for her next voyage. Captain Smith remained in command, and Honorio Martin had risen to fourth mate. Also returning were Jamaican boatsteerer George Brown, who would spend twelve years on board; William McKutchinson from St. Vincent, who signed on as preventer (backup) boatsteerer; and James Antone from Dominica. However, John E. D. Smith remained ashore, and the rest of the crew was new. Charles Stanton, from Pennsylvania, was both the ship's carpenter and the engineer for the steam engine; James Kennett, from New York, was blacksmith; and W. W. Whiting, twenty-five, from New York, was steward. James Marshall, thirty-seven, from Cabo Verde, was cook; William George, twenty-three, from the island of St. Helena, was cabin boy; and F. H. Roberts, eighteen, from Guam, served the idlers in steerage.

The *Morgan* departed San Francisco on December 3, 1887, to pass through the South Pacific, seeking sperm whales on the way to the Sea of Okhotsk. In March, the vessel reached Saipan in the Northern Mariana Islands. There, several deserters ran from the vessel, and there a stowaway hid himself on board. The stowaway was dropped off at Nagasaki, Japan, in April. At Saipan or Nagasaki, several new men joined the crew.

The *Morgan* then continued hunting sperm whales in the Sea of Japan before working north into the Sea of Okhotsk. While hunting bowheads there on September 7, a whaleboat capsized. In that cold water, far from home, James Antone and the young English recruit S. K. Pickersgill drowned. With the vessel bound for San Francisco on October 14, the thirty-year-old replacement blacksmith, Englishman George Williams, died of tuberculosis. Three weeks later, on November 5, the *Morgan* arrived with a cargo worth $20,327 (about $654,000 in 2023).

—◦◦◇◦◦—

Three weeks after arriving, the *Morgan* was ready to depart on its next voyage, with mate John S. Layton elevated to captain. Fourth Mate Honorio Martin was back, as was boatsteerer George Brown, cook James Marshall, cooper and carpenter Manuel F. de Limas, cabin boy William George, seaman William McKutchinson, and five others. Second Mate A. Spiering, thirty-three, had been born in the Dakota Territory and apparently made his way west, where he became a Pacific whaleman. Third Mate Antone Cabral, thirty-eight, was from Brava, Cabo Verde, while extra boatheader H. M. King, thirty-eight, was a throwback to the *Morgan*'s first voyage as a native of Edgartown. His presence suggests that the *Morgan* now carried five active whaleboats, or else the captain no longer lowered. Preventer boatsteerer Joseph Vincent, twenty-three, was one of five men from Guam on board, steward Edward Verbracken was from Antwerp, Belgium, and other men came from Chile, Peru, Mauritius, and Hawaii.

On the waterfront of San Francisco, maritime labor was unreliable. Shipping agents known as "crimps" might offer up a lot of misinformed and even "Shanghaied" men who were delivered drugged or dead drunk. And men themselves might attempt to obtain an advance, then abscond (or be Shanghaied) on another vessel. Between the time the *Morgan*'s crew list was filed at the customhouse and the time the vessel passed through the Golden Gate, nine men deserted.

After departing on November 26, 1888, the *Morgan* again headed south for sperm whaling. The vessel called at MacAskill Island—Pingelap in the Carolines—to obtain chickens, ducks, and coconuts, then stopped at Pohnpei (then called Ascension Island). From the Carolines the *Morgan* headed up to the Mariana Islands, stopping at Saipan. Among the islands, Captain Layton filled out the crew, and on April 12 they struck, but lost, the first whale of the voyage.

The *Morgan* called at Vladivostok on the Russian coast of the Sea of Japan in July before proceeding north to the Sea of Okhotsk. Along the way, one of the recent recruits, Aleck Kanaka, died on board. In the Sea of Okhotsk, the crew took five whales before heading into the Pacific on October 10. Three days later, another recruit, Dick Kanaka, died. Two weeks after that, on October 26, 1889, the *Morgan* entered San Francisco Bay with a cargo valued at $23,752 (about $789,275 in 2023).

———◦◇◇◇◇◦———

Captain Layton, now forty-four, remained in command as the vessel was prepared for another one-year voyage. Honorio Martin was now second mate, George Brown was back as a boatsteerer, Charles Stanton remained the carpenter and engineer, Edmund Verbracken returned as steward, George Williams continued as cabin boy, and John E. D. Smith rejoined the *Morgan* as cooper and carpenter. The new men came from a typical range of origins, from Wisconsin and Montana to Northern Europe, South America, and the many islands that sent men into the whaling industry. Again, nine men deserted before the vessel departed, but two men who had been signed for the Wings' bark *Cape Horn Pigeon* mistakenly joined the *Morgan*, though they did not receive the normal $50 advance.

The *Morgan* departed San Francisco on December 5, 1889. During the sperm-whaling cruise, several men deserted at the islands in February. In March, the vessel visited the Yellow Sea between China and Korea before heading into the Sea of Japan. On July 1, the *Morgan* was at Vladivostok on the Sea of Japan, where another man deserted. Captain Layton may have called there to seek a permit from the Russian government to whale in the bays on the west coast of the Sea of Okhotsk as Russian patrol vessels sometimes seized whaleships working near Russian coastal waters. The *Morgan* then sailed north into that sea.

On September 1, the larboard boat, with Second Mate Honorio Martin, boatsteerer William H. Griffith, and J. B. Cook, B. F. Hargrave, John Peters, and Tom Stephensen, struck a one-hundred-barrel whale. It towed them off on a classic "Nantucket sleigh ride" until they were out of sight of the *Morgan*. They lanced and killed the whale, then lay by it overnight, waiting for the *Morgan* to find them. The vessel did not appear. With only the lantern keg of hardtack and a small amount of water on board, they decided to abandon the whale and seek land. Martin knew that Sakhalin Island off the Russian coast was about one hundred miles west. Five days later, in famished condition, they reached Sakhalin and wandered inland seeking help. When they returned to the shore, they sighted the *Morgan* sailing away, having given up hope of finding them. Natives gave them some food and directed them to a settlement, which turned out to be a Russian convict camp. At first imprisoned under suspicion of spying, they eventually found transportation south to Hong Kong. There, they boarded a steamship and arrived at San Francisco on December 7, 1890, more than a month after the *Morgan* arrived to report them lost at sea.

The *Morgan* had arrived on November 8 after a very poor voyage, which would have been considerably improved if Martin's whale had been secured. As it was, the cargo was worth only $11,720 (about $393,000 in 2023). When the crew lined up for their pay, quite a few of the men received just one dollar, as the balance of their lays went to cover the cost and interest on their advances.

CHAPTER 9

Captain Earle Goes Whaling in a Changing World
1890–1904

As the son of a captain, James A. M. Earle of Edgartown, Martha's Vineyard, had gone to sea in about 1865 as an eleven-year-old cabin boy. Rising through the whaling ranks, he had made his reputation as a whaling captain in command of the bark *Splendid* when the crew recovered a large lump of ambergris worth $150,000. He would now take command of the *Charles W. Morgan*.

Three of the four mates, including Third Mate Simeon Leach, who had been fourth mate during the last voyage, were Massachusetts men. Again, there was a fifth boatheader or mate. George Brown returned as a boatsteerer, Charles Stanton was again carpenter and engineer, John Branscombe returned as cook, and John E. D. Smith, now fifty-six, was back for a last voyage as cooper. Steward Joseph Sablan, forty-three, of Guam, brought his seventeen-year-old son Felix along as cabin boy. The crew also included the vessel's first Japanese sailor, N. Matsutara, twenty-two.

The *Morgan* departed San Francisco on December 2, 1890, heading south to follow the pattern set by captains Smith and Layton. Less than a month out, seaman and preventer boatsteerer Enos Chaco of Guam died at age twenty-three. When the vessel arrived at Pohnpei (Ascension) in January, engineer Charles Stanton and two other men ran off, and another one deserted at Guam the next month. The *Morgan* worked the Yellow Sea, the Sea of Japan, and then the Sea of Okhotsk before returning to San Francisco on October 31, 1891, with a cargo worth $29,669 (about $997,000 in 2023).

Captain Earle, Second Mate William W. James, boatsteerer George Brown, and cook John Branscombe then made a similar voyage with an almost entirely new crew, departing on November 24, 1891, and returning on November 7, 1892. They found few whales, and the value of the cargo was just $10,644 (about $358,000 in 2023).

PHOTO BY DENNIS A. MURPHY. (MYSTIC SEAPORT MUSEUM, D2014-06-179)

———◇◇◇◇◇———

A month later, Captain Earle had resupplied and cleared the *Morgan* at the custom-house for another voyage. No longer was whaling a young man's occupation. Boat-header William H. Young was fifty—eleven years older than Captain Earle—and the three mates were forty-six, thirty-five, and twenty-nine. The boatsteerers were in their midtwenties to late thirties. One of them, German-born Harry A. Kluge, thirty-eight, had risen from seaman to boatsteerer over three voyages.

As had happened before, nine men ran off after the vessel was cleared at the customhouse but before it set sail on December 8, 1892. In July 1893, two men ran off at Guam, and later that month another six deserted in Japan.

As the season was ending in the Sea of Okhotsk, on September 10 the lookout reported an unfamiliar craft approaching. Captain Earle went aloft with a spyglass and saw what appeared to be an Asian coastal sampan with ten men on board. Captain Earle armed himself and ordered Mate Horace Tower to take their line if they came alongside but not to allow them on board. Through pantomime they expressed their hunger and thirst, and seaman John Jacobs of Alaska recognized their language as Russian. Acting as interpreter, he learned that they had escaped from the same prison camp where Honorio Martin and his boat's crew had been retained. Riding astern of the *Morgan*, the sampan rose on a wave and smashed one of the windows of the captain's cabin. Earle then ordered the men aboard and let the damaged sampan go.

The incident was symbolic of the political state of the Pacific in the 1890s. Here, a fifty-year-old American sailing whaleship owned in Massachusetts, with men from Scandinavia, Germany, Portugal, the United States, and the colonial outposts and many island cultures of the Pacific, encountered fugitive Russian political prisoners off the desolate coast of Siberia. A few days later, when the bark *Cape Horn Pigeon* sailed within sight, Captain Earle persuaded his friend Captain Thomas Scullun to take five of the fugitives.

The *Morgan* arrived back at San Francisco on November 9, 1893, with a small cargo worth just $10,949 (about $372,000 in 2023). Captain Earle tried to deliver the Russian prisoners to federal authorities, but no one chose to handle this unprecedented case. Reportedly, after a short time as attractions in a sideshow, they moved on. Three of them killed a farmer, then two of them turned on the third and killed him. Those two were tried and hung; the other seven disappeared from further scrutiny.

—◈◇◇◈—

Less than a month after arriving, the *Morgan* was resupplied and ready for the next voyage. George Brown returned as boatsteerer, but most of the rest of the crew was new. First Mate Frederic C. Swain, forty-six, was a Scotsman, and Fourth Mate Joe Avellar, thirty-three, was from the Azores. Two of the other boatsteerers were from Cabo Verde, and one was from Cuba. This time the carpenter and "donkey driver" (engineer) was Karl V. Ross, twenty-eight, from Finland.

At least four men deserted after the *Morgan* was cleared for departure. The vessel left without them on December 6, 1893. This time, Captain Earle intended to concentrate on sperm whales along the equator, near New Zealand and off Japan. The first stop was at Pohnpei (Ascension Island) in the Carolines, where two men were discharged for disability and two deserted in February.

The *Morgan* then sailed south to Auckland, New Zealand, where six men deserted on February 17. While there, possibly taking some instruction in navigation, forty-year-old Captain Earle was introduced to eighteen-year-old Honor Matthews. By the time he left, they were apparently talking of marriage.

The starboard bow boat approaches the *Morgan* as the vessel holds it position with main topsails filled and fore topsails aback. When the boat is aboard, the crew will use the fish tackle, with its two blocks, to hoist the anchor into position on the rail. (MYSTIC SEAPORT MUSEUM, 1983-2-16)

On July 27, the *Morgan* called at Hakodate, at the south end of the Japanese island of Hokkaido. Hakodate was the first Japanese port opened to foreign trade in 1854 after the US Navy expedition commanded by Matthew Calbraith Perry arrived in Japan to compel a treaty that opened the nation to trade after centuries of self-imposed isolation. Now Hakodate was a center for trade and had an international population. Five men deserted while the *Morgan* lay there to resupply.

A few weeks later, on August 18, 1894, First Mate Frederic Swain brought his boat up to a one-hundred-barrel bull sperm whale. When the boatsteerer darted his iron, the whale lashed out with his flukes, smashing the boat. Mate Swain must have been struck directly as only his hat remained among the wreckage of the boat, but the other members of his boat's crew were picked up by the other boats.

Later in 1894, the *Morgan* called at Rotuma in the Fiji Islands, making the last visit there by an American whaleship, concluding almost seventy years of regular contact between the islanders and whaleships. In October, the *Morgan* was back in New Zealand waters and apparently called at Norfolk Island, where at least eight recruits joined the crew. Among the descendants of the principal HMS *Bounty* mutineers living there were George, Gresley, Holder, and Parker Christian, descended from Fletcher Christian and his Tahitian wife Mauatua, and Albert, Hessie, Walter, and Willie Quintal, descended from Matthew Quintal and Tevarua. They may have seen the *Morgan* when it called there in 1887; now they were signed aboard.

After a second circuit of the western Pacific, the *Morgan* arrived back at San Francisco on November 5, 1895. The voyage had been successful enough to return $47,271 (about $1,720,000 in 2023) for the two years.

On December 2, the *Morgan* began its twenty-first voyage. Captain Earle was likely eager to depart as he had arranged to meet Honor Matthews in Honolulu, where they would be married. George P. Christian, forty, great-grandson of Fletcher Christian, had come aboard at Norfolk Island during the last voyage and was now first mate. The second and third mates were from the Azores, and the fourth mate was from Cabo Verde, while the boatsteerers, still including George Brown, were from the Azores, Cabo Verde, Jamaica, and Peru.

The *Morgan* arrived at Honolulu a few weeks later, and, on December 27, 1895, James A. M. Earle and Honor Matthews were married. She then moved aboard the *Morgan* as the fourth captain's wife to sail aboard. Reportedly, Captain Earle taught her celestial navigation and she made herself comfortably at home onboard. When they returned on November 1, 1896, Captain Earle delivered a cargo worth $14,197 (about $516,625 in 2023). He then settled his accounts, and he and Honor headed east to Martha's Vineyard.

———◦◇◇◦———

The Wings then recalled John S. Layton to take command. His first mate, Horace F. Tower, was fifty, and forty-five-year-old Honorio Martin was back as fourth mate. They departed on December 3, 1896, heading for Saipan and the coast of Japan for sperm whales before returning to the Sea of Okhotsk. In the Sea of Japan, they sighted and took their first whale on April 9.

When Captain Layton became ill, he directed the *Morgan* to Hakodate. While he was treated, Mate Tower attempted to take the *Morgan* on a short cruise. However, the vessel ran aground in the harbor and lay for two days until it could be hauled off. Then, on May 15, ten of the crew refused to work until the captain returned aboard. Mate Tower confined them in the hold with only bread and water, and when they were released on May 17 five of them deserted. A number of Japanese sailors were then enlisted, being entered phonetically on the crew list as Ishito-rationo, Sakuminta Kunkitan, Kemada Kuramruka, and Yokahama Ohasuki.

During a later call at Hakodate, the *Morgan* also signed on an extremely skilled whaleman. The Wings' bark *Cape Horn Pigeon*, also working in the Sea of Japan, was wrecked in July with the loss of nine hundred barrels of oil. The crew was saved, and at least one of the officers, Emanuel Morgan, then joined the *Morgan*. Emanuel Morgan was born on Mahé, Seychelles, in the Indian Ocean northeast of Madagascar and one thousand miles east of Zanzibar. Mahé is the principal island of the Seychelles group, which was settled by the French in the 1700s and then taken

Rigged for whaling in the Sea of Japan and Sea of Okhotsk, the *Morgan* awaits a breeze with almost all sails set. With both the lookout hoops above and a canvas-sided crow's nest at the top-mast crosstrees, the fore topgallant and royal yards have been removed. Notice the patched sails and the Pacific-style triangular spanker at the stern. A whaleman stands on the footropes as he works far out on the jibboom. For whaling in icy seas, the whaleboats have been painted in dark colors. (MYSTIC SEAPORT MUSEUM, 1945.452.20)

by the British. After years as a whaleman, Emanuel Morgan had risen to serve as a mate in the *Cape Horn Pigeon*. He would be associated with his new vessel for eight voyages over ten years.

After leaving Hakodate, the crew took at least eleven sperm whales, and in the Sea of Okhotsk they secured another four bowhead whales. On September 26, the *Morgan* passed Broutona Island, in the Kuril Islands between Japan and the Kamchatka Peninsula, as it left the Sea of Okhotsk. The next day the crew took down the canvas-sided crow's nest that had sheltered the lookouts from the cold wind. The *Morgan* arrived at San Francisco on October 25, 1897, with a good cargo worth $22,611 (about $830,000 in 2023).

———❖❖❖———

Captain Layton turned over command to Thomas Scullun, formerly of the *Cape Horn Pigeon*. Born at New Bedford in 1853—about the time the *Morgan* completed its third voyage—Scullun had gone to sea as a fourteen-year-old cabin boy and risen through the whaling ranks to take command of the *Cape Horn Pigeon* in 1888. On the *Morgan*, Captain Scullun had a very skilled set of mates and boatsteerers. His former mate, Emanuel Morgan, was first mate, George P. Christian was second mate, and Honorio Martin was third mate. The boatsteerers included George Brown, now forty; Peter Tatiano of Guam, thirty-eight; and two from Cabo Verde, Frank Matthews, forty-five, and Peter Layton, thirty. Engineer W. H. Summers of Maryland had been with the vessel for six years. Cook Carl Greton was from Germany, Steward Jose Santo was from Guam, and cabin boy Koto Walamak was from Japan. The seamen were a mix of men from Guam, Japan, Illinois, Iowa, Kansas, and Colorado.

After just seventeen days in port, the *Morgan* departed San Francisco on November 11, 1897. This voyage followed the usual pattern of cruising through the islands, up into the Sea of Japan, and concluding with a summer season in the Sea of Okhotsk. During a stop at Guam, probably in the spring of 1898, George Brown was paid off at Guam after twelve years and ten voyages as a boatsteerer aboard the *Morgan*.

During this voyage, the international balance in the Pacific changed dramatically. The United States declared war on Spain in April 1898 over the fate of Cuba and in the aftermath of the explosion of the USS *Maine* at Havana. In the Pacific, the US Asiatic Squadron entered Manila Bay in the Philippines on May 1 and defeated the Spanish fleet there. On June 20, a US Navy cruiser arrived to seize Guam. By the terms of the August 1898 peace protocol, Spanish possessions in the Caribbean and the Pacific were conveyed to US control. Enos Aflague, Lino Patricio, Peter Tatiano, and others began the voyage as Spanish citizens. They would return under American jurisdiction.

In June, Japanese seaman Takahasha died of tuberculosis on board. When the *Morgan* reached Hakodate in late July, one man was paid off and one deserted. Beyond that, it was a stable crew and a moderately successful voyage that ended on October 28, 1898 and produced $18,075 (about $666,000 in 2023).

Captain Scullun quickly prepared the *Morgan* for another voyage, departing on November 26. The officers, boatsteerers, and idlers remained largely the same, except that Thomas W. Swain, thirty-seven, of Tristan da Cunha, had replaced George Brown as boatsteerer. The voyage too was similar, ending on November 2, 1899, and producing $20,150 (about $742,000 in 2023).

Captain Scullun's third voyage in the *Morgan* began on December 7, 1899. His reliable mates remained, and this crew had a large contingent from Guam as well as cook Fidel Morris from Chile. Gregorio de la Rama from the Philippines was signed on as "steerage boy" to serve as waiter to the boatsteerers and idlers. Whaling along the equator and on the coast of Japan, the *Morgan* spoke with its sisters in the Wing fleet, the barks *California* and *Alice Knowles*. Most of the catch was taken in May and June. When on the coast of Japan, reportedly a ninety-foot whale rose under one of the boats, smashing it and depositing the men in the sea, unhurt. Another boat took the whale, which produced thirty-eight barrels. On

October 29, 1900, the *Morgan* landed oil and bone worth $17,684 (about $643,500 in 2023). In reporting to the media, Captain Scullun emphasized that the *Morgan* was "still sound and a good sailer."

—∞∞∞—

Captain Earle then resumed command. Emanuel Morgan was absent, but the other officers remained. The *Morgan* departed on November 22, 1900, and returned

The *Charles W. Morgan* lies on the busy San Francisco waterfront in November 1900, shortly before departing for its twenty-sixth voyage. The yards are swung, and the main yard is cockbilled to avoid tangling with the yards of the large merchant ships on either side. (IMAGE COURTESY OF THE SAN FRANCISCO NATIONAL MARITIME PARK)

on October 29, 1901, with a very good cargo worth $38,565 (about $1,387,000 in 2023). Captain Scullun then took over again, and Emanuel Morgan returned as first mate.

The *Morgan* departed on November 27, 1901, for the sperm-whaling grounds. Several times during the voyage the *Morgan* encountered pods of whales. Once, nine dead sperm whales lay alongside for cutting in, and twice they took five whales in a day. By the end of the season they had taken sixty whales. On August 18, 1902, Mate Emanuel Morgan recorded in the logbook: "we sight a large schools of Large sperms whale we saw whale all day long until night we did not lowered on account we are full ship it is to bad we are not 200 tons biggest what a chance for oil."

During the voyage, seaman Nelson Lambert, from Guadeloupe in the West Indies, was aloft painting the masts when he fell. He suffered a compound fracture of one leg, which Captain Scullun attended to with poor results. Lambert left the *Morgan* crippled, and he eventually settled in Providence, Rhode Island. Despite feeling that he had not been properly cared for, he would revisit the *Morgan* on several occasions during her eventual time as a museum ship.

On August 22, boatsteerer "John Perry"—probably John Peres—died. Morgan recorded, "at 5.30 John Perry pass away dead land bearing N. by E." The next day, he wrote, "we came to give John Perry a Burial." Four days later, he added, "we sold John Perry personely effect at auction for $10.00[.] 75¢ in his purse." That was in accord with the tradition of selling a dead sailor's possessions to his shipmates.

When they returned to San Francisco on October 28, 1902, the $34,289 cargo (about $1,200,000 in 2023) was almost as valuable as the one from the previous voyage and more than double the return from five of the previous eleven voyages.

In 1902, Captain Earle returned to the *Morgan*, accompanied by Honor and their three-year-old son Jamie. In the captain's stateroom, there was now a small bathtub, a great convenience for a wife and child. Jamie originally slept on the wide transom behind the sofa in the day cabin, but the vessel's motion often rolled him off his mattress. Captain Earle then had a hanging box bed set up in the day cabin, where Jamie slept comfortably. During the day, Honor Earle might take him up to the roof of the hurricane house for a view of the sea and the sailors at work. Except in special circumstances, he was restricted to the after deck, aft of the mainmast, like his mother. Jamie Earle idolized Second Mate George Christian, who often spent time with him and made him toys.

Captain James M. Earle (1854–1935) was the *Morgan*'s longest-serving master, making nine voyages, totaling ten years, between 1890 and 1907. During the 1895 voyage, he married Honor Matthews (1874–1949), who made several voyages and sometimes served as navigator. Their son James W., "Jamie," sailed with them on the 1902–1903 voyage. Here they stand near the boat skid deck, with a couple of officers working aft near the mizzenmast. (MYSTIC SEAPORT MUSEUM, 1973.899.231)

Captain Earle poses with Jamie on the hurricane house at the *Morgan*'s stern. Jamie sits on the shelf for the larboard running light, where a red lantern would be displayed at night. (MYSTIC SEAPORT MUSEUM 1975.383.34)

With the tryworks smoking, Jamie Earle plays the whaleman. At left, a man uses a mincing knife on the mincing horse to cut a horse piece of blubber into "bible leaves." In the background, a whaleman uses a long-handled metal bailer to pour hot oil from the try-pot into the large copper cooling tank behind Jamie. Between the metal smokestacks of the tryworks is a metal cresset, which could be filled with burning blubber scraps and hung between the stacks to provide light when trying out at night. The tarp is rigged to shelter the try-pots from rain. (MYSTIC SEAPORT MUSEUM, 1975.383.31)

Standing between the mizzenmast and the door to the deck cabin built for Mrs. Tinkham, Jamie Earle shows off his toy gun. He spent eleven months on board, playing on deck in good weather and sleeping in a swinging bed in the captain's day cabin. He idolized Second Mate George P. Christian, who built him a toy boat and often played with him. (MYSTIC SEAPORT MUSEUM, 1975.383.42)

With his hat and toy pistol, Jamie Earle poses near the windlass with four of his "shipmates" of varying ethnicities. (MYSTIC SEAPORT MUSEUM, 2009.22.89)

Again seeking sperm whales—one of very few vessels still hunting them in these waters—the *Morgan* headed for the Marquesas Islands south of the equator, where the vessel had last called back in 1868. Then it headed for the Bonin (Ogasawara) Islands, one thousand miles northwest of Guam and six hundred miles south of Japan. After time on the Japan grounds, the *Morgan* returned to San Francisco on October 27, 1903. The cargo was worth $26,614 (about $925,000 in 2023).

With the price of oil and bone dropping, despite the still economically viable supply of whales in both the Arctic bowhead-whaling and Pacific sperm-whaling grounds, whaling agents were refiguring their vessel management. In San Francisco, labor costs had risen as whale products dropped in value. There, the crimps and boardinghouse masters had cornered the business of supplying crews. Captain Earle had to pay $1,200 in "blood money" to the crimps to obtain a crew for his next voyage. And, though whaling sailors had long been prone to deserting, the sailors assembled for crews in San Francisco were especially unreliable, often deserting after receiving their advance but before the vessel departed. Even one year of whaling for a lay rather than a specified wage was no inducement to San Francisco sailors, except for skilled men or for islanders with few other options.

The *Morgan* departed San Francisco on November 18, 1903. On this voyage, the fourth mate was Richard L. McLachlan of New Zealand. Nine years later, when the city of New Bedford wished to create a monument to celebrate its whaling past, sculptor Bela Lyon Pratt would use McLachlan as his model for a boatsteerer darting his iron. The sculpture, "A Dead Whale or a Stove Boat," stands in front of the New Bedford Free Public Library.

The *Morgan* again visited Guam on the way to the Japan grounds. While the vessel was in those waters in early February, an Asian conflict erupted. Japan had been developing its military and contesting both China and Russia on the Asian mainland since 1894. At the same time, Russia was aiming to seize a year-round port on the Yellow Sea, west of Korea. When negotiations failed, Japan declared war on Russia and the Japanese navy attacked and blockaded Russian forces at Port Arthur through the spring. In August, the Japanese fleet would turn back the Russian fleet in the Yellow Sea. Though fought outside the Sea of Japan, the conflict threatened the normal maritime activities around Japan.

The *Morgan* arrived at San Francisco on October 31, 1904, with a catch worth $26,319 (about $900,000 in 2023), which William Wing calculated at a very good $62.98 per day for the 347-day voyage. Captain Earle then turned over command and took the train east.

——◦◦◇◇◦◦——

While the *Morgan* was repeating traditional patterns of whaling under sail, the industry was changing. In 1863, the Norwegian whaler Svend Foyn had built the first steam-powered whaling vessel, and, in the United States in 1865, the New

Somewhere in the Pacific Ocean, the *Charles W. Morgan* steps along under nearly full sail. Notice the Pacific-style spanker with narrow head and the laundry hung to dry in the rigging above the whaleboats. (MYSTIC SEAPORT MUSEUM, 2009.22.15)

London, Connecticut, whaler *Pioneer* was fitted with a steam engine for propulsion in the eastern Arctic ice. Gradually through the 1870s, the design for steam whalers was refined, with strengthened hulls and efficient engines. The last whaling bark, the *Wanderer*, was launched at Mattapoisett in 1878, and thereafter only steam-powered whalers, with auxiliary sailing rigs, were added new to the fleet.

In the 1850s, whaling technology was expanded by Captain Thomas Welcome Roys, who had first opened the Arctic bowhead grounds in 1848. Bomb lance guns were then being adopted in the fleet, and Roys experimented with guns before developing a whaling rocket to hunt fast-swimming rorqual whales. Since they often sank, he developed a steam-powered winch to haul them to the surface. For the same purpose, the Norwegian Svend Foyn perfected a harpoon cannon in 1868.

European whalers also expanded the hunt to Antarctic waters, which few American whaleships visited. These waters were home to many rorquals—blue, finback, and humpback whales especially. While the *Morgan* was hunting sperm whales under sail in 1904, Carl Anton Larsen set up a Norwegian whaling station on South Georgia Island, using harpoon cannons on steam-powered hunter boats. The operation took almost two hundred rorquals the first year and almost thirty thousand within ten years.

CHAPTER 10

Return to New Bedford
1904–1913

William R. Wing had decided to bring the *Charles W. Morgan* back to New Bedford. To command the vessel, Wing engaged sixty-year-old Captain Edwin J. Reed. Born in South Dartmouth, Massachusetts, just west of New Bedford, Reed had gone to sea in 1860 and was a captain by 1878. Emanuel Morgan remained as first mate, but the other mates were new men from Cabo Verde in their twenties, John Pereria, who had advanced from boatsteerer, Antone Alameda, and Antone Silva. The foremast hands were new.

The *Morgan* made its last departure from San Francisco on November 25, 1904, already short three men who "failed to report for duty when ship sailed." Within a few weeks, the other men became contentious as the vessel headed for the Pacific sperm-whaling grounds.

Congress had occasionally passed acts to prohibit the worst abuses of seamen, both at sea and ashore, but sailors themselves had little control over their daily lives. As American labor increased the effort to organize and unionize in the decades after the Civil War, the National Seaman's Union of America was founded in 1892 to advocate for sailors' rights. Yet, the union recognized the need for unquestioning discipline in the sailor's workplace at sea, where obeying orders without question could be a matter of life and death. So, like other oppressed workers, sailors might engage in petty resistance. In the early 1900s, ongoing labor strife among railroad workers and coal miners, and the "muckraking" journalists who publicized corporate oppression, increased the chances that labor issues would surface on the *Morgan*. The officers might lump both troublemakers and activist sailors under the term "sea lawyers," but some sailors had enough knowledge of the law and a desire to assert rights, even aboard a wandering whaleship. Captain Reed may have anticipated the difficulties to come, as he kept a second log documenting the behavior of the crew, written in the form prescribed by federal authorities. Both Captain Reed and Mate Morgan signed the entries.

Ohio-born Charles King, twenty-five, seems to have been a ringleader. The mate learned that King was planning to disobey until the officers used force, then sue them in court when the vessel reached port. When King stood up to the mates, he was put in irons until he relented. Then "Juan Avis" and "Lewis Almeda"—who don't appear in the crew list under those names—refused an order from Mate

Shadows on the main staysail. PHOTO BY DENNIS A. MURPHY. (MYSTIC SEAPORT MUSEUM, D2014-06-1083)

Morgan, claiming they were off watch. They were also confined in irons until they promised to return to duty. Petty obstruction continued until the *Morgan* arrived at Norfolk Island in May 1905. There, King and three young greenhands deserted but were unable to hide on that small island and were recaptured and confined until they agreed to return to duty. However, a Coloradoan named Rose remained defiant, and in June Mate Morgan grabbed him by the collar and shook him—without striking him, as the captain attested.

Next, the ship's carpenter, Adolph Koch of Germany, refused the mate's order to repair a pump, and a few days later he attacked Mate Morgan with an ax, for which he was disarmed and restrained. Manuel Rosa then defied the mate's order to go aloft and was put in irons. With this defiant behavior continuing, Captain Reed brought the *Morgan* to Tahiti in August to confer with the American consul, W. F. Daly. The consul took testimony and then sentenced Koch and Rose to jail on Tahiti until after the *Morgan* departed. The crew list recorded Koch's dismissal for "insubordination" and Rose's by "mutual consent." Meanwhile, ten new men were signed on.

While the *Morgan* was whaling in the eastern Pacific in December 1905, Theodore Roosevelt and other naturalists met in New York City to create the American

Bison Society and set up protected reserves on the Great Plains in which to preserve the bison from extinction. This was likely the world's first effort to establish
refuges in which to rehabilitate and conserve an endangered species. Since then,
the bison population has risen to five hundred thousand, or five percent of its once
vastness, and the concept of protected reserves has been applied at sea as well.

In January 1906, Charles King again defied the mate, refusing to turn out when
his watch was called and then cursing and threatening the mate. He would spend
two days in double irons. Once around Cape Horn, the *Morgan* headed north to
call at Barbados in April, where three men deserted and three signed on. While
whaling in the Atlantic in May, Charles King and nine other men refused to man
the boats when a whale was sighted. As the end of the voyage was near, Captain
Reed threatened to confine them in irons for the rest of the voyage.

Despite the recurring difficulties throughout the 564-day voyage, the *Morgan*'s
hunt for whales had been moderately successful. When the vessel arrived at New
Bedford on June 12, 1906, the cargo was worth $20,294 (about $692,000 in 2023),
which William Wing calculated as $35.94 per day. But the vessel had returned
to a very different New Bedford. More than twenty large mills of the expanding
textile industry, employing thousands of men and women, now drove the local
economy and brought increasing prosperity to the city. The whaling industry still
claimed a small portion of the waterfront, but whaling under sail was now a mar-
ginal industry.

—◦◦◯◦◦—

Nevertheless, the Wings planned that the *Morgan* would return to its previous
grounds in the South Atlantic and Indian Ocean. To command the vessel, they
requested that James Earle, now fifty-two, come over from Martha's Vineyard. He
and Honor arrived to make the voyage together, and on August 11 the *Morgan*
departed. The captain's old shipmate George Christian was on board as second
mate and John Pereira had returned as third mate. First Mate Judson A. James of
Falmouth, Massachusetts, thirty-nine, had recently returned from a voyage in the
bark *Josephine*. During the voyage, Honor Earle would act as assistant navigator.

Not long after the voyage began, Manuel Rosa, a troublemaker from the previous
voyage who was still aboard, got into a fight with Third Mate Pereira, injuring the
mate's hand badly enough that he was off duty for several days. Captain Earle confined Rosa in irons for a week. But then trouble developed with First Mate James,
who repeatedly second-guessed the captain's decisions. The other mates, except
for George Christian, also proved troublesome.

The *Morgan* had success whaling off the Crozet Islands in the winter of 1906–
1907, and in April Captain Earle took the vessel to Durban (Port Natal) on the
east coast of South Africa. Founded in 1824 at the site of a Zulu settlement on
a well-sheltered harbor, Durban became an increasingly important port under

With sails set for drying—including the Pacific-style spanker with narrow head—the *Charles W. Morgan* lies at New Bedford's Central Wharf. Notice the small wooden structure with sliding door next to the wharf shack. It appears to be an obsolete camboose or galley house of the type the *Morgan* carried on the larboard foredeck before construction of the hurricane house galley at the stern. (MYSTIC SEAPORT MUSEUM, 1985-6-120)

George Parkin Christian (left) and Antone J. Alameda stand near the carpenter's bench on the *Morgan*'s deck, ca. 1906. A grandson of *Bounty* mutineer Fletcher Christian, George Christian grew up on Norfolk Island and signed aboard the *Morgan* in 1893. Between 1893 and 1913 he made twelve voyages, usually as boatsteerer or second mate. Antone Alameda, from Cabo Verde, served as fourth mate for the 1904–1906 and 1906–1908 voyages. (MYSTIC SEAPORT MUSEUM, 1977.280)

British rule in South Africa. There, the crew unloaded the oil and baleen for shipment home. Captain Earle discharged the first and third mates, three boatheaders, and several sailors, while Manuel Rosa and other sailors deserted there. With new mates and several new crew members, and fresh supplies for another season of whaling, the *Morgan* departed for another cruise. But, before he left, Captain Earle wired the Wings, asking to be relieved of command. His health, and the difficulty of managing the crew, had convinced him to return home early.

The Wings sent out sixty-five-year-old Captain Hiram Nye of North Falmouth, Massachusetts, to assume command. He arrived at Durban on a steamship on about July 19, 1907, to meet the *Morgan*. James and Honor Earle took a steamship home and after one more voyage on the Wing bark *Alice Knowles*—during which they had their younger son Norman on board—they retired ashore to Quincy, Massachusetts. James A. M. Earle would live until 1935.

Captain Nye took the *Morgan* up to the Mozambique Channel, between Madagascar and the east coast of Africa, and then down to the Crozet Islands. From there, the *Morgan* passed the Cape of Good Hope and worked its way up the South Atlantic, watching for whales. The vessel called at Cabo Verde and at the Azores before returning to New Bedford on the Fourth of July 1908. Only about ten of the original crew of about thirty-six returned with the vessel. Between the oil and bone sent home and the further take, the voyage returned $34,082 (about $1,137,000 in 2023).

A country boy, born in Granville, Massachusetts, in 1859, Arthur O. Gibbons had commanded mostly small whaling brigs and schooners. Now he took command of the *Morgan* at the age of forty-nine. New York–born Joseph Thurston, now fifty-nine, returned to the *Morgan* as second mate, having made seven voyages as fourth or third mate between 1897 and 1904, and George Christian was back as a boatheader, possibly commanding a boat in place of the captain.

Departing on September 2, 1908, the *Morgan* again headed for the Indian Ocean to whale among the Crozets in their warmer months of December through February before heading north to the east African coast. This crew was more tractable, and the voyage went smoothly until the *Morgan* called at Durban, South Africa, in April 1909.

While at Durban, cooper-carpenter Carsten and engineer-blacksmith Rasmussen both died and Captain Gibbons fell ill. He remained ashore while the *Morgan* made a cruise under the new first mate, Joseph Roderick. As neither Roderick nor the other mates were proficient at celestial navigation, William Haggie joined the crew as navigator.

Deciding that he was too ill to return to the vessel, Captain Gibbons wired the Wings to request a replacement captain. They selected Captain Charles S. Church. Charles Church had been born at Acushnet, near New Bedford, in 1864, and at age eighteen was a seaman in the bark *Niger*. When he was whaling out of San Francisco, he met and married Charlotte Ott, the daughter of a San Francisco harbor pilot. They came to New Bedford when he brought the bark *Andrew Hicks* back from San Francisco. Now the two of them would take a steamship to Durban to join the *Morgan*. A generation younger than Lydia Landers, Clara Tinkham, and Mrs. Keith, Charlotte "Lottie" Church—like Honor Earle—was a modern woman who wished to have a role in assisting her husband and not simply to accompany him as a passenger.

When Captain Church took command, Mate Frederick Roderick was discharged and a new mate Senna was engaged, but he quickly proved erratic and was discharged as insane. Third Mate Nicholas Francis was elevated to first mate, but Lottie Church acted as assistant navigator and took over the duty of keeping the

Charlotte "Lottie" Church and Captain Charles S. Church pose on the *Morgan*'s after deck in their shoregoing clothes, ca. 1911. After joining the vessel at Durban, South Africa, in 1909, they would complete the voyage in 1910 and return for a second voyage, 1911–1913. (MYSTIC SEAPORT MUSEUM, 1973-3-549)

logbook. Her entries would be far more detailed than usual, noting the standard latitude, longitude, and course, but adding distance sailed each day, variation, barometer and thermometer readings, the wind force, sea state, and weather. Regularly she placed notes in bottles, indicating the vessel's name, position, and weather conditions when she released them.

Her log entries sometimes included bits of shipboard detail. One of her first entries recorded the death of the vessel's aged cat, Major. When the steerage cat gave birth to a kitten, she noted "an addition to the ship's crew." On June 25, 1910, she wrote: "killed fourteen scrawny chickens tonight. The whole lot won't make a good dinner." She expressed her dry humor on occasion, noting in August 1910, "We have two live pigs, one rooster, four cats? and almost twenty canary bird—no fear of starving for a while." As she suffered from asthma, she was solicitous of the crew members who became ill during the voyage.

A crew member remembered Captain Church as very strict about shipboard protocol but still a kind master. At Christmas, he gave each man a jar of marmalade, an unusual treat for a sailor at sea.

After time on the African coast and a return trip to the Crozets, the *Morgan* returned to the Atlantic and made its way back to New Bedford, arriving on September 12, 1910. The cargo was valued at $34,272 (about $1,107,000 in 2023), an average of $46.31 per day for the 740-day voyage.

⎯⎯∞∞⎯⎯

Since 1887, the *Morgan* had followed a routine with only a month, or occasionally two, between voyages. The crews maintained the vessel at sea, but there was no time for a major overhaul. This time, the Wings spent almost seven months to make repairs and, probably, caulk the vessel and recondition its bottom.

For the next voyage, Charles and Lottie Church returned to the *Morgan* as captain and assistant navigator. George Christian was back as second mate, with William H. Griffiths as first mate. Griffiths would keep the log, though Lottie Church continued to assist with navigation.

The voyage began successfully, with seven hundred barrels of oil taken in the Atlantic. However, less than three months into the voyage, cook Isaac Joab died on September 5. Mate Griffiths recorded, "At 8 a.m. called all hands Mr. Christian read him a funeral sermon and he was buried from the starboard gangway with all respect of our crew."

When the *Morgan* called at Faial on the way south, a number of the crew deserted, "being men who did not know what whaling was when they left home," according to Lottie Church. Continuing south, they took a right whale and several sperm whales near Tristan da Cunha before heading for the Crozets. This season, they found no whales there.

The *Morgan* arrived at Durban on April 13. There, the crew tarred the rigging and resupplied for the coming cruise. On April 17, Mate Griffiths noted that all the vessels in the harbor had their flags at half-mast in tribute to those who had been lost on the *Titanic* five days earlier. At Durban, several men were punished for fighting and three men deserted but returned before the *Morgan* sailed.

The vessel then sailed up the Mozambique Channel and on to the Seychelles, northeast of Madagascar. In those waters, the crew took enough whales to produce one thousand barrels of oil. They took on provisions at Bird Island and Mahé in the Seychelles before heading north to cruise for whales along the Arabian coast. They then beat against the wind on the way back down the Mozambique Channel and arrived at Durban in October. There, Captain Church authorized the replacement of the boiler tubes in the *Morgan*'s twenty-six-year-old donkey engine. During the layover at Durban, Mate Griffiths noted that boatsteerer Manuel Claudino went ashore on Sunday, November 5, and "was arrested for being sober!" The Wings considered Claudino "a good boatsteerer and a reliable man," so this seems to be a bit of sailor humor.

The *Morgan* departed Durban on November 30, 1912, and spent the next five months on the African coast. On March 29, 1913, the crew took a sperm whale, and when cutting in the next day they discovered more than fifteen pounds of amber-gris, which was worth $1,154 (almost $36,000 in 2023).

In May, the *Morgan* arrived at the island of St. Helena, where several men were recruited to fill out the crew. One of them, Frederick Young, began to show signs of insanity. One day he climbed down to the chain bobstay under the bowsprit and refused to return to the deck. The crew had to haul him back on board. A few days later he caused a commotion, for which Captain Church confined him in irons in the blubber room. While harmless to his shipmates, he upset the routines during the last months of the voyage.

The *Morgan* arrived back at New Bedford on August 9, 1913. The price of sperm-whale oil had dropped from 63 to 43 cents per gallon during the voyage, but with three thousand barrels of oil and the ambergris, the cargo was valued at $39,749 (about $1,232,000 in 2023), averaging $48.41 (about $1,500 in 2023) per day for the 821-day voyage.

"I believe the owners are going to refit her in the spring—she is quite an old vessel and considered a very lucky ship and is very comfortable," wrote Lottie Church to a friend. However, the Wing firm was in transition. Original partner William R. had died in 1908, and the youngest brother, John, was now eighty (he would die in 1915). William's son-in-law Charles Morgan Hussey—Charles W. Morgan's grandson through his daughter Elizabeth Rodman Morgan Hussey—was also in management, but he was not moved to refit his grandfather's namesake vessel. The firm had the *Morgan* stripped of sails and equipment and towed across the harbor to lie at Union Wharf in Fairhaven. The Wings would send their bark *Andrew Hicks* to sea in 1917 to make the firm's last voyage after sixty-five years of whaling-vessel ownership. Charles Morgan Hussey would sell their outfitting business to the Steiger-Dudgeon department store in 1923, closing out the history of J. & W. R. Wing.

CHAPTER 11

Last Days of Whaling Under Sail
1916–1921

Back in 1903, some prominent New Bedford residents had assembled to establish the Old Dartmouth Historical Society to focus on the region's history, especially its whaling history. The organization grew quickly, and in 1907 it opened a museum in a donated bank building on Water Street. In 1915, Emily Bourne donated a large new building in memory of her whaling-agent father, Jonathan Bourne Jr. The next year the museum installed a fully rigged, eighty-nine-foot half-scale model of Bourne's bark *Lagoda*, which had been built in 1826, converted to a whaling vessel in 1841, and broken up in 1899. While a

The *Charles W. Morgan* under full sail, August 2014. PHOTO BY DENNIS A. MURPHY (MYSTIC SEA-PORT MUSEUM, D2014008-0408)

Captain Benjamin D. Cleveland (1844–1925) poses with his pet dog in the captain's day cabin the evening before the *Morgan* departed in September 1916 for its thirty-fourth voyage. (MYSTIC SEAPORT MUSEUM, 1963.536.6)

few aged whaling vessels like the *Morgan* might still be seen on the waterfront, this pristine model represented them to the visiting public.

But, even as the *Lagoda* model took shape, the *Morgan* received a reprieve from abandonment. Captain Benjamin D. Cleveland needed a vessel. Benjamin Cleveland was born at Edgartown, Martha's Vineyard, in 1844 and went to sea in 1876. By 1900, his commands and financial interests were in smaller brigs and schooners that specialized in hunting elephant seals at the Desolation (Kerguelen) Islands in the south Indian Ocean.

The smaller sealing industry had existed alongside the whaling industry since the late 1700s. After fur-seal populations were decimated, sealers moved into the islands near the Antarctic, seeking seals for oil. Of the seals, the large, aggressive elephant seal became the most intensively hunted, especially by vessels from New London, Connecticut. The Desolation Islands became the focus of the hunt.

Located one thousand miles east of the Crozets, almost two thousand miles southeast of Madagascar, and three thousand miles southwest of Australia, the Desolation Islands were well named as one of the most remote locations on earth. Sighted by a French explorer in 1772, the windy, cold, desolate island group was being visited by sealers within a decade.

As pursued by American sealers in the 1800s, the hunt took place on land. The crews often set up camp and a tryworks on the beach. Some of the crew wielded guns or long killing lances to attack and stab the huge seals in the heart or lungs. Others used long knives to strip the carcasses of the skin and the blubber. The blubber was sometimes tried out on shore, and the oil was barreled and carried out to the vessel. Otherwise, the blubber was boated out to the vessel and rendered in the tryworks there. The thick seal skin was salted and packed for processing into industrial leather. In an industry largely pursued in remarkably small schooners, the *Charles W. Morgan* would be unusually large.

In 1916, the *Morgan* was hauled out on a Fairhaven marine railway for some caulking and bottom work. Notice the thin sheets of copper covering the bottom to discourage boring "shipworms" and marine growths. On the stern, just under the A in CHARLES, a white ring marks the outlet for the officers' head (toilet) in the hurricane house on deck. This view also shows off the fine lines of the "run," as the hull narrows from the greatest width amidships to the rudder at the stern, enhancing the smooth, speedy passage of the hull through the water. PHOTO BY ALBERT COOK CHURCH. (MYSTIC SEAPORT MUSEUM, 1971-11-29)

After three years of layup, the *Morgan* also received a new coat of paint. From this perspective, the bow looks extremely blunt and boxy, but below the waterline it is shaped to combine the buoyancy of a wide bow with a smooth flow through the water. Notice how the two iron hawsepipes have been worn by the anchor chains during seventy-five years of service. (MYSTIC SEAPORT MUSEUM, 1971-12-150)

This starboard perspective shows the finer shape of the *Morgan*'s bottom. The lower of the two pipes through the topsides near the foremast is for the fluke chain that was wrapped around a dead whale's tail to secure it alongside. PHOTO BY ALBERT COOK CHURCH. (MYSTIC SEAPORT MUSEUM, 1971-11-33)

Preparing to depart in September 1916, the crew works at the pump-break windlass to raise the light larboard bower anchor. At left, one of the crew uses a hook to pull lengths of anchor chain off the windlass for stowage in the chain locker in the hold. The large block at right is part of the fish tackle for hoisting the anchor onto the rail, where it will be lashed like the heavier best bower anchor at lower right. The ship's bell is mounted on top of the heavy pawl post, the attachment point for the wooden pawl that falls into the notches in the windlass to prevent it from turning back. (MYSTIC SEAPORT MUSEUM, 1994.53.97)

Captain Cleveland and his investors paid about $6,000 to purchase a 60/64 share of the vessel from the Wings, the other 4/64 share remaining in William R. Wing's estate. Captain Cleveland held a 24/64 share as the managing owner. The new owners did as little maintenance as possible, even using cement to patch some rotten spots. Then the vessel's old sails, packed away for three years, were bent on for another voyage.

Before departing, the *Morgan* was chartered by a film company to serve as a setting for a silent film based on the 1902 novel *Miss Petticoats*, which starred the popular Alice Brady. The film included scenes on a whaling ship, and the producers were very happy to find an actual one. They affixed a new nameboard, Harpoon, and paid some of the outfitting fees and a lease fee. The film was released at the end of July, even before the *Morgan* went back to work.

In preparation for an extended period at the stormy Desolation Islands, Captain Cleveland had a roof built over the tryworks. After time on a marine railway to check the bottom, refasten the copper, and clean it, the *Morgan* departed New Bedford on September 5 to seek whales on the way to Desolation. The crew had the usual mix of whalemen, plus a small group of young adventurers from Boston. They sighted the first whale on September 20 and lowered three boats but could not dart a harpoon. Two days later they sighted a pod of sperm whales and again lowered three boats. The bow boat succeeded in killing its whale, but the waist boat was stove and lost its whale, and the larboard boat lost its whale when the iron drew out.

They took whales on two more occasions before the *Morgan* reached São Vicente, Cabo Verde, on November 9. Despite their success, the *Morgan* was not in good shape. "The ship started leaking after the first storm by the time we reached here she was leaking like a basket," wrote one of the young Boston men when they reached Cabo Verde. They refused to continue and contacted the American consul for a survey. The *Morgan* crossed to Brava, where a few repairs were made. However, the Boston group had had enough and fled to the hills, hiding until the vessel departed.

The *Morgan* came in sight of the Desolation Islands on February 11, 1917, but it took ten days to beat to windward and reach them. There, they anchored and began their bloody work. All progressed routinely until April 19, when Captain Cleveland recorded phonetically,

> About 10 o'clock a.m. very moderat whether but the see was very bad Boats went on shoor to bring of eliphant bluber and the surf riased up and turned one boat over and lost 4 men Ther names Richards Moor Aguste Lemas Albert Rubeiro and Daniel O'conor The rest of the crew on duty at Desolation Island.
>
> Signed: Benjamin D. Cleveland master
John D. Lopes cheffe mate
Charles Johnson boatsteerer

—◦◦◇◦◦—

The *Morgan* left the Desolation Islands on May 12 and headed back to the South Atlantic, reaching St. Helena on August 8. The vessel lay there for eight days to resupply, take on water, make some repairs, and give the watches liberty on shore. They sailed on August 16, bound for the West Indies, and arrived at the island of Dominica on September 23. They continued on to St. Eustatius and St. Barthélemy, and somewhere in the islands Captain Cleveland learned that the United States had entered the world war in April. Cleveland later suggested they barely avoided hitting an explosive mine near Dominica, but there is no record of this in the logbook. Sailing apprehensively along the coast, they arrived at New Bedford on October 23, 1917, with a cargo valued at $21,000 (about $500,000 in 2023).

The *Morgan* lies at a New Bedford wharf with sails hoisted for drying, probably at the end of the 1916–1917 voyage to the Desolation Islands. The larboard whaleboats rest in the water while the spare boats still rest bottom-up on the boat skids. (MYSTIC SEAPORT MUSEUM, 1983-11-22)

With the United States now fully involved in the war, Captain Cleveland decided to sell his share of the *Morgan*. However, he would remain engaged in the industry until his death in 1925. His share of the *Charles W. Morgan* went to Captain John A. Cook. Born at Provincetown, Massachusetts, in 1857, Cook had been whaling since the 1870s. Since he registered the vessel at his home port of Provincetown, the *Morgan* would carry that as the hailing port inscribed on the stern, but Cook fitted the vessel out in New Bedford, and it departed from there on July 16, 1918. Captain Cook had engaged Joseph F. Edwards as master. Born at Flores in the Azores, he had served as a preventer boatsteerer for the *Wanderer*'s 1913 voyage. Now he was master of the *Morgan*.

Trying to avoid German U-boats, Captain Edwards took the *Morgan* to the West Indies and then to the Brazil Banks off South America. They found whales there, and, when the *Morgan* returned to New Bedford on September 7, 1919, the cargo of 1,150 barrels of oil was worth more than $25,000 (about $430,000 in 2023).

Prices for whale products remained firm, even though a postwar recession would soon set in. To take advantage of the present market, Captain Edwards took the *Morgan* out again about five weeks after arriving. They headed for Cabo Verde to fill out the crew, then headed for the South Atlantic, taking about 750 barrels of oil. Seven months out, Captain Edwards became ill enough to take to his berth. Mate Peter B.

All painted up and with the sails in a tight harbor furl, the *Morgan* lies at anchor off Fairhaven in New Bedford Harbor. At left is the 1878 whaling bark *Wanderer*. PHOTO BY A. F. PACKARD. (MYSTIC SEAPORT MUSEUM, 1939.1242)

The larboard waist boat comes alongside as the *Morgan* departs New Bedford in July 1918. The fore and main courses are clewed up and ready to be set when the wind picks up. Notice that vessel now has hoops on both fore- and mainmasts and the main royal yard has been sent down. (MYSTIC SEAPORT MUSEUM, 1983.22.149)

Alves, a whaleman of long experience, decided to bring the vessel home so the captain could be treated. They arrived on July 16, 1920. With the economy now declining, the 750 barrels of oil were worth less than $9,000 (about $135,000 in 2023).

Captain Cook found a most experienced captain for the next voyage. Captain John Theophilo Gonsalves had been born at Brava, Cabo Verde, in 1858 and went to sea aboard the New Bedford whaler *Roman* as cabin boy at age eleven, rising through the ranks. Departing on September 9, 1920, Captain Gonsalves took the *Morgan* to the West Indies whaling grounds, but crew trouble broke out. When they called at Dominica, a number of crew members deserted and a mix of young landsmen, including tailors' apprentices and clerks, signed on as a way to reach the United States. But first they learned to whale, and during the voyage they took many sperm whales.

On May 21, 1921, 79 1/2 years after taking its first whale, the *Charles W. Morgan* cut in its last whale. A week later, the *Morgan* arrived at Provincetown to report its arrival, then sailed on to New Bedford with 2,702 barrels of oil. During the war, oil had sold for 75 cents a gallon, but in the postwar recession it was down to 30 cents a gallon. Though large, the *Morgan*'s last cargo was valued at just $25,534 (approximately $434,000 in 2023). This last cargo, taken in eight months, exceeded the size of the *Morgan*'s first cargo, taken in forty-one months, by three hundred barrels, but, due to the decline in the value of sperm-whale oil, the first cargo's value in 2023 dollars exceeded the value of the last cargo by $1,750,000.

Through eighty years, the *Charles W. Morgan* traveled nearly a million miles. At least a thousand men served aboard the vessel, some for a few months, some for years. A few men were lost, a few died on board, and many deserted, but overall the *Morgan* had been a lucky, well-managed vessel and was considered comfortable by one of the five captains' wives who had made their homes on board. But New Bedford's whaling industry was almost done. Captain Cook laid up the *Morgan* again at Fairhaven, and the vessel's last master, Captain Gonsalves, would eventually return to Brava, where he would die in 1928. Only eighteen traditional American whaleships remained active, and they made only forty-one voyages after the *Morgan*'s last departure. The schooner *John R. Manta* would make New Bedford's last successful whaling voyage in 1925, and the US industry in its traditional form would end at San Francisco in 1928.

When the *Charles W. Morgan* completed its thirty-seventh voyage, the United States spanned the continent with forty-eight states and 106 million people, presided over by President Warren G. Harding. Eighty years earlier, when the *Morgan* was launched, the nation lighted its homes with spermaceti candles and whale-oil lamps, lubricated its machinery with whale oil, and used baleen for its elastic properties. Whaling was considered the nation's fifth-most-important industry. Now, electric lights had largely replaced candles and oil lamps, petroleum products supplied power and lubrication, and celluloid and spring steel had supplanted baleen. During the vessel's eighty years at sea, nineteen presidents had served, twenty-two states had joined the Union, and the population had grown by seven hundred percent. The nation was now an industrial giant rather than a maritime power.

CHAPTER 12

Museum Ship
1922-THE PRESENT

Hesitant to put money into the maintenance of a vessel with few prospects, the *Morgan*'s owners let the vessel lie while they considered options. The *Morgan* had already appeared in a film, and now another opportunity arose. Elmer Clifton, who had worked for the D. W. Griffith studio, was making a popular film with a whaling theme, to be titled *Down to the Sea in Ships*. Prominent actors William Walcott (as "Charles W. Morgan"), Marguerite Courtot (as his daughter Patience), and Raymond McKee (as her love interest) would play major

Artist Harry Neyland (1877–1958) painted the *Charles W. Morgan* lying at Fairhaven in 1925. By that time, Neyland was the vessel's "master and managing owner" and was seeking funds to preserve the vessel as a museum. (MYSTIC SEAPORT MUSEUM, 1974.7)

Clara Bow, as "Dot," is discovered in a try-pot in the *Morgan*'s blubber room in the 1922 film *Down to the Sea in Ships*. (MYSTIC SEAPORT MUSEUM, 1988.63)

The earliest photograph of the *Morgan*'s fo'c'sle, with worn bunks and companionway ladder just aft of the foremast, was taken during the filming of *Down to the Sea in Ships*. (MYSTIC SEAPORT MUSEUM, 1986-6-112)

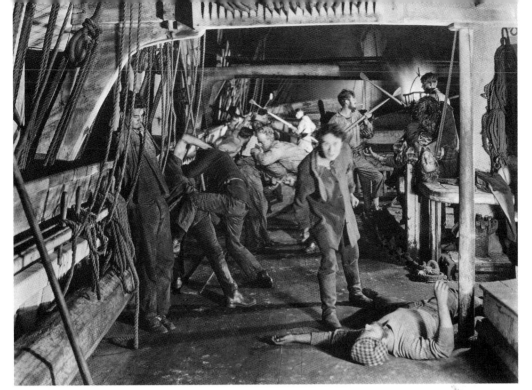

This fight scene from *Down to the Sea in Ships* shows the deck little changed from the *Morgan*'s last whaling voyage a year earlier. In this view forward from under the boat skids, the cutting irons still rest in the overhead rack and a rough spar timber is lashed along the rail. (MYSTIC SEAPORT MUSEUM, 1976-6-81)

roles, and young Clara Bow, later known as the "It Girl," would be featured as Morgan's granddaughter Dot.

Clifton engaged the *Morgan* as a setting for many scenes. For the film, the vessel was rerigged to a degree as a full-rigged ship again. However, the actual sailing scenes for the film were taken of the whaling bark *Wanderer*. The whaleboat scenes were filmed from the motor schooner *Gaspee* on the West Indies whaling grounds. The film debuted at New Bedford's Olympia Theater on September 25, 1922. The townspeople were thrilled to see their history on the screen, and the film went on to a popular run worldwide.

Soon after, the Paramount film studio planned a film version of Joseph Hergesheimer's popular 1920 novel *Java Head*. The *Morgan* was taken up to Salem, Massachusetts, to portray the 1840s East India merchant ship *Nautilus*. The film was directed by George Melford and starred Leatrice Joy, Jacqueline Logan, Alan Roscoe (as the *Nautilus*'s captain), and Frederick Strong. The eighty-minute film was released on January 28, 1923. No copies are known to have survived.

The *Morgan* was then taken back to New Bedford and laid up across the harbor in Fairhaven. There the vessel attracted the attention of Harry Neyland, an American impressionist artist who had come to New Bedford in 1911. Neyland viewed the *Morgan* as a possible city or state history museum and began buying shares of

The burned-out steamer *Sankaty* lies alongside the *Morgan* at Fairhaven in July 1924. The Fairhaven Fire Department extinguished the fire before it spread to the *Morgan*. (MYSTIC SEAPORT MUSEUM, 2000.100.86.805)

the vessel. By 1924 he owned a 27/32 share of the *Morgan* and was listed as master and managing owner.

His efforts almost went up in flames that year when the steamer *Sankaty* caught fire at a New Bedford wharf and drifted across the harbor, coming to rest against the *Morgan*'s port quarter. Fortunately, the Fairhaven fire department extinguished the fire before the *Morgan* suffered anything more than scorched paint.

Neyland was unsuccessful in persuading city, state, or federal authorities to preserve the *Morgan* for the public, so he turned to Colonel Edward Howland Robinson Green, son of Hetty Green and grandson of the *Morgan*'s former owner Edward Mott Robinson. Green was an enthusiastic man with several hundred million dollars from his mother's estate. He had recently completed a large mansion on his 240-acre estate, Round Hill, on the shore of Buzzards Bay, southwest of New Bedford. In 1925, Neyland and Green incorporated Whaling Enshrined "to enshrine and preserve the whaleship, *Charles W. Morgan*, and other relics of the whaling industry; to create and foster an interest in the history of whaling and the trades that are subsidiary thereto; . . . and generally to discover, procure and preserve whatever may relate to general history and antiquity."

As president and treasurer, Green provided the funding to build a cofferdam at Round Hill, where the *Morgan* could be imbedded in sand; to move the vessel there; and to outfit it with sails and open it for exhibition. Still rigged as a full-rigged ship and flying the house flags of the many New Bedford whaling firms, the *Charles W. Morgan* was dedicated as a museum ship in 1925. Although there is no firm evidence that the *Morgan* ever had the painted gunports on its topsides that some whaleships

With a ship rig and painted gunports, the *Charles W. Morgan* went on exhibit in a sand berth at Round Hill near New Bedford in 1925. Morris Rosenfeld captured visitors inspecting the ship that year. (MYSTIC SEAPORT MUSEUM, © ROSENFELD COLLECTION, 1984.287.17269F)

displayed, at Round Hill the *Morgan* was painted with them. Soon, the *Morgan* and the Round Hill exhibits became a popular destination for tourists out in their automobiles. For "captain," inter- preter, and shipkeeper, Green and Ney- land found whaling captain George Fred Tilton of Martha's Vineyard, who had first gone whaling in 1875 and later com- manded steam whalers.

—◦◦◦◦◦—

While the *Morgan* had become a symbol of a whaling industry past, after World War I, industrial whaling expanded. In 1923, the first factory ship, equipped to both kill and process whales, arrived in Antarctic waters. The next year, the more efficient factory ship *Lancing*, with

Captain George Fred Tilton (1861–1932) was born on Martha's Vineyard and first went whaling in 1875. He later commanded steam whalers in the Western Arctic and in retire- ment acted as the *Charles W. Morgan*'s captain and interpreter at Round Hill. Here he stands by the vessel's windlass and bell. (MYSTIC SEA- PORT MUSEUM, 1961.229)

The 1938 hurricane shifted the *Morgan* in its sand berth and damaged it slightly, leaving it beyond the ability of Whaling Enshrined to restore it. (MYSTIC SEAPORT MUSEUM, 2009.22.79)

a stern ramp to haul out dead whales for processing, set a new standard for factory ships. Within five years, and just before the Great Depression, the Antarctic whalers would kill 40,201 whales in one year.

The Great Depression began to impact Round Hill's success about the time Captain Tilton died in 1932. Already Colonel Green had been losing enthusiasm in the project, and when he died in 1935, Harry Neyland and the other supporters discovered that he had left no provision for the *Morgan* in his will. They were still trying to raise money for the vessel in September 1938 when a great hurricane struck New England without warning. The force of the waves lifted the *Morgan* partly out of its sand bed and left it damaged but still sound.

Carl C. Cutler (1878–1966) had made a voyage under sail before becoming a lawyer and then a maritime historian. In 1929, he and two friends established the Marine Historical Association at Mystic, Connecticut, and ten years later the organization was seeking a ship for its growing museum. Cutler handled the negotiations with Whaling Enshrined to preserve the vessel at Mystic. (MYSTIC SEAPORT MUSEUM, 1949-2-7)

Down in Mystic, Connecticut—a former shipbuilding port that had sent some whaleships to sea—a group similar to Whaling Enshrined was seeking a ship for their growing museum. Carl C. Cutler, a lawyer turned maritime historian who had briefly gone to sea under sail, had joined with two friends to establish the Marine Historical Association on Christmas Day in 1929. They too believed the artifacts and history of the nation's seafaring past were being lost in the industrial present and sought to preserve some of it. By the late 1930s, they had exhibits in a former textile mill built by the shipbuilding Greenman brothers and were about to expand onto the site of the Greenman shipyard.

In November 1941, the *Charles W. Morgan* was towed up the Mystic River and through the bascule bridge as it approached its new berth at what was becoming Mystic Seaport Museum. (MYSTIC SEAPORT MUSEUM, 1966.5.54)

To celebrate its one hundred and first birthday in July 1942, the *Charles W. Morgan* was bedecked with signal flags and the house flags of New Bedford whaling firms. (MYSTIC SEAPORT MUSEUM, PN-227A)

Carl Cutler approached Whaling Enshrined to discuss the acquisition of the *Charles W. Morgan*. While the New Bedford community opposed the loss of such an important piece of local history, no funding was forthcoming there. When Cutler provided assurances that the Maritime Historical Association had the resources to preserve the vessel, the *Morgan*'s supporters reluctantly agreed to let it go. "Ashes to ashes, Dust to Dust, If Mystic don't take her, The Devil Must," wrote the supporters.

Finally patched and hauled from the sand berth, the *Morgan* was towed by a US Coast Guard cutter to Mystic. On November 8, 1941, the vessel came up the river and through the bascule highway bridge with a group of Sea Scouts on board. Only a month later, the attack on Pearl Harbor launched the United States into World War II. Had the *Morgan* not left Round Hill when it did, it likely would have gone to pieces through neglect during the war.

At Mystic, the *Morgan* was filled with large ballast stones and set in sand. Wooden piers provided access for the many visitors who came to

GAMMING
Used for lifting the captains wife aboard and lowering her into a small boat to go 'gamming'— (visiting with another whaleship).

"GAMMING CHAIR"

For years, this gamming chair was exhibited on deck to represent the captains' wives who sailed on the *Morgan* and may have used such a chair to be lifted in and out of whaleboats when "gamming," or visiting another whaleship at sea. (MYSTIC SEAPORT MUSEUM, PN-227A)

see the vessel, even during the war. After the war, the Marine Historical Association provided regular care. The association was popularly named Mystic Seaport as it brought representative buildings to its waterfront to create a nineteenth-century "seaport" for visitors. These buildings included the James Driggs shipsmith shop, which had produced whaling ironwork on the New Bedford waterfront before joining the *Morgan* at Round Hill and now Mystic Seaport. During these years, shipwrights shaped a number of new spars and gradually rebuilt the *Morgan*'s topsides. Working on the stern in 1957, they discovered the evidence of the original four stern windows, which had later been replaced by two port holes.

Museum shipwrights rebuild a portion of the *Morgan*'s bow in 1950 as the vessel rests securely in a bed of sand. (MYSTIC SEAPORT MUSEUM, 1950-8-53)

Nelson Lambert, the last-known survivor of the *Morgan*'s crews, poses at the wheel fifty-five years after sailing aboard in 1901–1902. A native of Guadeloupe, Lambert broke his leg in a fall from aloft and blamed the officers for the poor treatment that left him crippled. (MYSTIC SEAPORT MUSEUM, 1957-9-8)

In 1967, the *Charles W. Morgan* was declared a National Historic Landmark under the program overseen by the US Department of the Interior. With the responsibility to maintain this nationally important artifact, Mystic Seaport Museum authorities faced decisions about the vessel's long-term preservation. After doing detailed surveys of its condition and considering the ways historic vessels were preserved elsewhere—in sand berths, in dry docks, on supports in buildings, or afloat—the Museum's staff and trustees concluded that it would be best to refloat the *Morgan* and maintain it in the water rather than as a land-based structure.

Trustee Henry B. du Pont provided generous funding for the restoration shipyard that bears his name at the south end of the Museum. Planned by Waldo Howland, a descendant of New Bedford whaleship owners and a shipyard owner himself, and marine engineer Maynard Bray, the yard was fully equipped with a large ship saw, a lathe for turning long spars, jointers and planers, and shipwrights skilled in the use of the broadax and adze. The shipyard also featured a cable-operated lift dock capable of lifting the *Morgan* and all of the Museum's other vessels out of the water for service.

By 1961, the *Morgan*'s stern had been rebuilt with the earlier four windows. PHOTO BY LOUIS MARTEL. (MYSTIC SEAPORT MUSEUM, 1961-8-118)

John F. Leavitt (1905–1974) had served in coasting schooners as a young man before becoming an artist and marine historian. He came to Mystic Seaport Museum as the *Morgan*'s shipkeeper in 1960, and here he shows two young visitors the tryworks in 1963. Leavitt would write the first full history of the *Morgan* in 1973. PHOTO BY SANDY DEVEAU. (MYSTIC SEAPORT MUSEUM, 1963-9-39A)

Perhaps inspired by an article on the Museum in *National Geographic Magazine*, a long queue of visitors climbs the *Morgan*'s gangway, passing under the cutting stage, which is lowered into the position for cutting in a whale. (MYSTIC SEAPORT MUSEUM, 1970-9-195)

In December 1973, the sand berth that had contained the *Morgan* since 1942 was carefully excavated until the vessel floated free on a high tide. Notice that much of the topside planking had been replaced by 1973 while the bottom planking was still largely original. PHOTO BY MARY ANNE STETS. (MYSTIC SEAPORT MUSEUM 1973-1104)

Howard Davis spent decades working on the *Morgan* as a Mystic Seaport Museum shipwright. Here he recaulks the bottom planking during the vessel's restoration in 1974. PHOTO BY KEN MAHLER. (MYSTIC SEAPORT MUSEUM, 1974-1-299)

Below the *Morgan*'s stern, shipwright Elwood Bogue uses a shipwright's adze to fair the edge between the vessel's deadwood and the new false keel as the vessel is restored on the Museum's lift dock. Most of the *Morgan*'s structural timbers were originally shaped by adzes like this. PHOTO BY KEN MAHLER. (MYSTIC SEAPORT MUSEUM, 1974-7-108)

Under the direction of the shipyard's new director, Maynard Bray, the *Morgan*'s hull was carefully excavated, and, on December 6, 1973, the vessel floated once again. The bottom planks, which had been buried in sand for most of fifty years, were found to be in remarkably good condition. Hoisted on the lift dock on January 7, 1974, the *Morgan* spent about six months under restoration. The bottom was recaulked and resheathed, and a band of copper sheets was applied along the waterline to represent the former copper-sheathed bottom. The false keel and keel shoe beneath the original keel were replaced, but most of the vessel's timbers were considered sound. Research in records, photographs, and previous condition surveys indicated that it would be most accurate to restore the *Morgan* to its later period, after the deck structures had been moved to their present positions, a refit well documented in photographs. When the vessel was relaunched and rerigged in 1975, it was once again a double-topsail bark with black topsides without painted gunports. Shipwright Willets Ansel researched and built a new set of whaleboats for the vessel.

While the *Morgan* was at the du Pont Restoration Shipyard, a granite-faced wharf representative of the whaling wharves of New Bedford was built where the vessel had formerly rested in sand. Named Chubb's Wharf, it had three one-hundred-foot faces, so the *Morgan*, or any of the Museum's other vessels, could lie in different orientations for even weathering. In June 1974, the *Morgan* was rededicated at its authentic new wharf.

The restored vessel was outfitted with a new set of sails, sewn by Nat Wilson in the Mallory Sail Loft, an 1839 sail loft building that had been moved to the Museum from downtown Mystic. Twenty years later, the *Morgan* would receive another set of sails sewn in the Mallory Sail Loft by Australian sailmaker Don Lucas and Museum shipwright Gary Adair.

In 1968, *National Geographic Magazine* had published an article on Mystic Seaport Museum, which brought summer crowds to the Museum for years thereafter. Partly to engage those in the long line waiting to board the *Morgan*, the Museum created its Marine Outdoor Demonstration Squad. With the *Morgan* now at Chubb's Wharf, the "Mod Squad" would demonstrate sail-setting, whaleboat-handling, and other traditional maritime skills on and around the vessel.

The *Morgan* also figured as a film location again. In 1972, it was used for deck scenes in the TV movie *The Man Without a Country*, starring Cliff Robertson and Beau Bridges. In 1978, the vessel was a backdrop for scenes in the PBS version of the Eugene O'Neill play, *Mourning Becomes Electra*.

During a major restoration between 1977 and 1984, shipwrights rebuilt the topsides, the main deck, and the stern and replaced the sternpost and stem. During this time, shipwright Henry Jarvis attended to the *Morgan* daily, and caulkers Howard Davis, Elwood Bogue, and Frank Raposa as well as shipwrights Arnold Crossman, Basil Tuplin, Roger Hambidge, and others spent many hours on projects on board.

With a new deck laid in 1979, Basil Tuplin (left) and Roger Hambidge use caulking irons and mallets to drive oakum into the seams while Henry Jarvis (right) seals the caulked seam with hot pitch. (MYSTIC SEAPORT MUSEUM, 1979-5-57)

In the hold, several frames were replaced from inside to preserve the original planking. During the final part of the restoration on the shipyard lift dock, the bilges were flushed and a number of artifacts, including buttons, clay pipe bowls, crockery, oil-lamp fragments, and a sperm-whale tooth, were recovered.

When relaunched in October 1983, the *Morgan* had a new tryworks, hurricane house, boat skid deck, skylight, and forecastle companionway. The stern had been rebuilt with two portholes again in place of the stern windows and with a simpler pattern for the gold eagle on the

Artifacts recovered from the *Morgan*'s bilge in 1982 included a sperm-whale tooth, clay pipe bowls, oil-lamp fragments, and buttons. PHOTO BY MARY ANNE STETS. (MYSTIC SEAPORT MUSEUM, 1982-11-118)

Standing near the *Morgan*'s rebuilt stern in 1985, role-player "Mrs. Talbot" tells a young visitor about the life of a captain's wife left ashore. In the background, the Marine Outdoor Demonstration Squad interprets the use of a whaleboat. (MYSTIC SEAPORT MUSEUM, 1985-8-68)

stern. Wishing to more accurately reflect the color scheme used in around 1900, the Shipyard Documentation Shop had done research and determined that ochre, not white, was the correct color for the inner surface of the bulwarks and other deck structures.

From 1986 to 1991, the quarters, fore and aft, were restored or rebuilt. Still images from *Down to the Sea in Ships* provided evidence for bulkheads, bunks, and woodwork treatment. In 1987, the vessel again spent time on the lift dock for replacement of the ceiling (inner) planks and the pointers that brace the bow in the lower hold. When relaunched, the *Morgan* was outfitted with a reproduction of the deck cabin built for Mrs. Tinkham in 1875 and removed in 1922. A new windlass was installed with fittings representing the connection to a steam-powered donkey engine.

For its hundred and fiftieth anniversary in 1991, the *Morgan* was fitted out with the whaling gear, provisions containers, textiles, and crockery that would be used for a voyage. Up forward, the forecastle was reconfigured with twenty-four rather than eighteen bunks, providing a more realistic view of the daily life of the *Morgan*'s sailors. The vessel also became a performance space for an annual public reading of *Moby-Dick* on Herman Melville's August 1 birthday.

In 1997, the *Morgan*'s blubber room in the 'tween decks represented the hold of a slave-carrying vessel in the Steven Spielberg film *Amistad*. For that film, with Djimon

The *Charles W. Morgan* provides an ideal setting for the annual public reading of *Moby-Dick* on Herman Melville's birthday. Here, an actor from the Theater of the Deaf reads a chapter in 1990. (MYSTIC SEAPORT MUSEUM, 1990-1455)

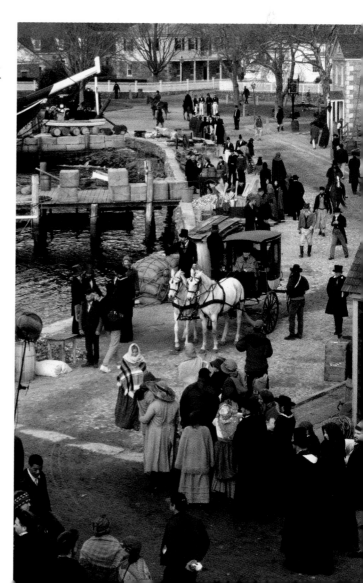

Hounsou as Cinque, leader of the captives, the Museum's waterfront was dressed to represent a bit of the New York waterfront in 1839. By the late 1990s, at least fifteen million visitors had boarded the *Morgan* since its arrival at Mystic Seaport Museum, sailing on countless voyages of imagination into the American maritime experience. Since then, annual maintenance and periodic hauling for care of the *Morgan*'s bottom continued. In the 2000s, a new round of restoration would begin.

In 1997, the Mystic Seaport Museum waterfront represented the New York waterfront for the film *Amistad*. The *Morgan* (top left) was undergoing restoration but still served as a location during the filming. PHOTO BY MARY ANNE STETS. (MYSTIC SEAPORT MUSEUM, 1997-286)

During the decades that the *Charles W. Morgan* has been a museum vessel, public perception of whales and our connection to them has gradually evolved. It is estimated that about 250,000 sperm whales had been killed by the time traditional American whaling came to an end in 1928. The right-whale population had been so reduced that the whaling nations instituted a ban on its further hunting in 1937. But, while the *Morgan* initially lay on exhibit at Mystic Seaport Museum, the industrial whaling fleet of the world went back to work after World War II with great efficiency. The International Convention for the Regulation of Whaling was held in 1946 and established the International Whaling Commission (IWC) to oversee the whaling industry across the world. Between 1946 and the 1980s, about 750,000 sperm whales, as well as many more rorquals, were shot and butchered by the factory ships. Alarmed at the slaughter, conservationists engaged

Although they did not operate on the scale of industrial whaling stations in Antarctic waters, Azorean whalers also processed their catch on shore. Here, at a whaling station on the island of Pico, a large sperm whale is prepared for processing, ca. 1960. (MYSTIC SEAPORT MUSEUM, 1965.889.1)

with the United Nations Conference on the Human Environment to call for a ten-year moratorium on whaling in 1972. In 1982, the IWC voted to institute a moratorium, and since 1987 most nations have abided by it. In the Azores, the open-boat whaling inspired by New England whaleships came to an end in 1984. In the United States, the Marine Mammal Protection Act of 1972 and the Endangered Species Act of 1973 have provided protection for whale species in the nation's waters.

As scientists have learned far more about the natural history of whales than the whalemen ever knew, many people have found a new fascination and affinity for these great creatures. Now, whale-watching boats and efforts to save stranded whales have replaced efforts to harvest them. A healthy population of gray whales attracts spectators as it migrates along the West Coast, and most of the world's fourteen populations of humpbacks have rebounded and the species now totals about forty thousand whales. Sperm whales are proliferating, now numbering perhaps 850,000, but the right whale, which was easier to catch and swims nearer to human activity, remains endangered, too often struck by passing ships or becoming entangled in fishing gear. Only about four hundred remain in the North Atlantic and perhaps two hundred in the North Pacific, though the more remote southern population is a good deal larger. The bowhead population had been reduced to about 3,000 by 1921, but has since increased to perhaps 50,000, although only a few hundred remain in the Sea of Okhotsk.

With the clear decline in the whale population and in the stocks of commercially important fish like cod and haddock through the 1960s, there was an obvious need to regulate commercial harvesting in US waters—especially with the establishment of the two-hundred-mile exclusive economic zone in 1982. After the establishment of the National Oceanic and Atmospheric Administration (NOAA) in 1970, Congress established the National Marine Sanctuaries under NOAA management in 1972. Several new sanctuaries were created when the act was reauthorized in 1992; these included the Gerry E. Studds Stellwagen Bank National Marine Sanctuary between Cape Cod and Cape Ann. There, humpbacks, finback whales, and smaller cetaceans feed and gather on the surface, now attracting whale watchers rather than whale hunters.

CHAPTER 13

The Thirty-Eighth Voyage
2014

After more than thirty years afloat on exhibition, with hundreds of thousands of visitors coming aboard each year, and periodic restoration projects, the *Charles W. Morgan* was due for a major condition survey and restoration in 2008. The vessel was hauled on the new lift dock at the Museum's Henry B. du Pont Restoration Shipyard in November 2008, and Museum shipwrights determined

The *Charles W. Morgan* on its way to its old home port of New Bedford during the thirty-eighth voyage. **PHOTO BY ANDY PRICE. (MYSTIC SEAPORT MUSEUM, 2014-07-1073)**

that perhaps half of the original bottom planks and frames had become seriously weakened after more than 165 years. The degree of rebuilding necessary—which would retain about twenty percent of the original material—would make the vessel seaworthy for the first time since 1920.

Museum authorities had always considered it too risky, and a disappointment to Museum visitors, to take the *Morgan* away from the waterfront to sail again. But the Museum's new president, Steve White, was willing to consider what might be gained, as well as what might be lost, by sailing the *Morgan*. Clearly such an endeavor would attract a worldwide audience who could watch from home, then support or visit the Museum in person. Visiting New England ports with a history of whaling—especially the *Morgan*'s original home port of New Bedford—would build strong bonds to the vessel and to the Museum. And operating the *Morgan* under sail would be a laboratory of square-rig ship-handling, teaching a new generation how to sail such a vessel. If properly undertaken, the risks could be managed. Following a feasibility study, the Museum's Board of Trustees voted on September 26, 2009, to approve a ceremonial thirty-eighth voyage.

Museum shipwrights Barry Rhodes and Trevor Allen assess the planks in the "run" near the stern. Note the tightly packed frames, some of which had been replaced. PHOTO BY DENNIS A. MURPHY. (MYSTIC SEAPORT MUSEUM, D2012-03-0618)

Under the supervision of Vice President for Watercraft Dana Hewson and Ship-yard Director Quentin Snediker, the vessel remained on land for almost five years as shipwrights shaped and installed replacement timbers and planks, almost always of the same species as the wood they replaced. More than thirty individuals, assisted by many volunteers, worked on the vessel. During their work, the vessel was fully interpreted for Museum visitors through exhibits and physical access when possible. When they were done, the *Morgan* was as "good as new." On the anniversary of its launch 172 years earlier, the *Morgan* was relaunched on July 21, 2013. Charles W. Morgan's great-great-great-granddaughter Sally Bullard rechristened the vessel with a bottle containing a mix of water from the seas the *Morgan* had sailed, plus a bit of rum.

While the vessel was under restoration, in 2010 the National Whaleboat Project was launched among American maritime museums to construct whaleboats

Looking like new, the rebuilt *Charles W. Morgan* rests on the Museum's lift dock while a crowd onshore and on the water awaits its relaunch. PHOTO BY DENNIS A. MURPHY. (MYSTIC SEAPORT MUSEUM, D2013-07-061)

Charles W. Morgan's great-great-great-granddaughter, Sally Bullard, breaks a bottle on the *Morgan*'s stem as the vessel is relaunched on July 21, 2013. PHOTO BY ANDY PRICE. (MYSTIC SEAPORT MUSEUM, D2013-07-0615)

that might be taken on the thirty-eighth voyage. Nine museums and boatbuilding schools contributed to the *Morgan*'s new "fleet" of ten whaleboats. They included Independence Seaport Museum in Philadelphia, the New Bedford Whaling Museum in collaboration with the Beetle Boat Shop (which had developed the Beetle model of whaleboat in around 1850), the Lake Champlain Maritime Museum in Vergennes, Vermont, and the Alexandria Seaport Foundation in Virginia. The boatbuilding programs included the Apprenticeshop of Rockland, Maine; Rocking the Boat of Bronx, New York; Lowell's Boat Shop in Amesbury, Massachusetts; the Great Lakes Boat Building School in Cedarville, Michigan; and the Gannon & Benjamin Marine Railway of Vineyard Haven, Massachusetts. Nine of the ten boats were built to the traditional Beetle pattern of New Bedford whaleboat (the other was modeled on the lines of a boat thought to have been built by Ebenezer Leonard of New Bedford). All of the boats had arrived at Mystic Seaport Museum by the spring of 2014, and each would be carried for part of the planned voyage.

For the sake of safety, the *Morgan*'s hull was equipped with a generator and electric bilge pumps, with a diesel-powered backup pump for firefighting as well as pumping out the vessel. The vessel was also outfitted with an electrical system to power the new fire and safety alarms, an electronic navigation system, and communications equipment. Modern water storage and marine sanitation systems supplanted the old water casks and over-the-side waste disposal.

Four of the key figures who made the *Morgan*'s thirty-eighth voyage possible pose during the sea trials. They are (left to right) Dana Hewson, vice president of watercraft preservation and programs at Mystic Seaport Museum; Captain Kip Files, the vessel's twenty-second captain; Nat Wilson, sailmaker from East Boothbay, Maine; and Quentin Snediker, director of the Henry B. du Pont Preservation Shipyard at Mystic Seaport Museum. PHOTO BY ANDY PRICE. (MYSTIC SEAPORT MUSEUM, D2014-06-0873)

A new set of spars was shaped in the du Pont Restoration Shipyard, and a new set of sails was sewn by Nat Wilson with the assistance of Mike Bartles in East Boothbay, Maine. To handle those, a crew of fifteen professional sailing mariners was assembled. Kip Files of Rockland, Maine, was selected as captain. With more than thirty years at sea, and time as captain of the 1877 bark *Elissa* of Galveston, Texas, as well as his own three-masted passenger schooner *Victory Chimes* in Maine, he had the experience and personality for the position. The crew included three mates,

Captain Kip Files conns the *Morgan* from the top of the hurricane house as the vessel is towed out of New London in June 2014. PHOTO BY DENNIS A. MURPHY. (MYSTIC SEAPORT MUSEUM 2014-06-0404)

The *Morgan*'s crew and some of the "38th voyagers" pose on deck before the sea trials off New London in June 2014. PHOTO BY ANDY PRICE. (MYSTIC SEAPORT MUSEUM, D2014-06-0872)

an engineer, and a cook, and it was filled out by a rotating group of experienced Museum staff members who normally set the *Morgan*'s sails and demonstrated the use of the whaleboats for Museum visitors.

The crew also contained eighty-five "38th voyagers," each of whom would sail aboard for one leg of the voyage. They included scientists, historians, writers, artists, actors, musicians, Herman Melville scholars, and others who could communicate the varied aspects of the experience to the public. "Stowaway" Ryan Leighton remained aboard for the entire voyage to post on a daily blog and social media.

Museum staff members would also set up a large dockside exhibit in several of the ports where the *Morgan* was opened for visitors. Featuring a life-size inflatable sperm whale

"Stowaway" Ryan Leighton uses twenty-first-century technology to Skype with members of Congress from the *Morgan*'s deck during the voyage. PHOTO BY DAN MCFADDEN. (MYSTIC SEAPORT MUSEUM, D2014-06-1092)

The tugboat *Sirius* comes alongside to take the *Morgan* "on the hip" and maneuver in Newport Harbor. At right is one of the swift tenders that assisted throughout the voyage. PHOTO BY DENNIS A. MURPHY. (MYSTIC SEAPORT MUSEUM, D2014-06-0688)

nicknamed "Spouter," the exhibit outlined the *Morgan*'s history and the whale species it had hunted and offered hands-on activities, demonstrations of maritime skills, and music and theater performances.

The Tisbury Towing tugboats *Sirius* and *Thuban* of Martha's Vineyard towed and tended the *Morgan* through the voyage, sometimes assisted by the Thames Shipyard tug *John Paul*. The *Morgan* was first towed about seven miles west to New London, the third-ranking American whaling port, for final outfitting and ballasting.

For three days in June 2014, the crew learned how to sail the *Morgan* during sea trials in Long Island Sound. They found that, despite its boxy appearance, the vessel was quite fast and maneuverable. It tacked (turned its bow through the wind) reliably and wore (turned its stern through the wind) with ease. The vessel could be held in position with the foresails aback, and Captain Files even figured out how to box-haul it, a backing-and-filling maneuver used by square-riggers to change tacks in confined waters. In heavier winds, the *Morgan* sailed well with just the fore-and-aft staysails. The *Morgan*'s performance confirmed remarks from the logbooks and was a tribute to those who designed and built it. "Those shipwrights in 1841 sure knew what they were doing," remarked Captain Files.

Under sail for the first time since 1921, the *Morgan* moves through Long Island Sound in June 2014. PHOTO BY DENNIS A. MURPHY. (MYSTIC SEAPORT MUSEUM, 2014-06-0607)

While tacking through the wind, the foresails have just been braced around to swing the bow. The main sails, now aback, will then be braced round to move off on the new tack. The *Morgan* proved to be as nimble as ever. PHOTO BY DENNIS A. MURPHY. (MYSTIC SEAPORT MUSEUM, D2014-06-17)

After the sea trials, on June 15 the *Morgan* was towed through Fishers Island Sound and then sailed up the Rhode Island coast to Newport. After three days there, the vessel was towed to open water and then sailed up Vineyard Sound and docked at Vineyard Haven on Martha's Vineyard, paying a ceremonial visit to the island from which had come six of its captains and many crew members.

On June 25, the *Morgan* left Vineyard Haven and passed through the Elizabeth Islands to sail across Buzzards Bay and once more enter New Bedford Harbor under sail, something the vessel had not done since 1921. The shores were lined with townspeople welcoming the *Morgan* home. Although the waterfront had changed greatly since 1921, the vessel would lie at a wharf not far from where it lay during its whaling days.

After two weeks at New Bedford, the *Morgan* was towed into Buzzards Bay, where it sailed to the Cape Cod Canal. From there, it was towed through the canal, then sailed across Massachusetts Bay to the former whaling port of Provincetown, the port whose name the vessel carried on its stern in 1918–1921 and visited briefly in 1921. The *Morgan* was moored off the waterfront, alongside the support vessel *Mystic Whaler.*

For those on board, the highlight of the voyage was the three cruises to the Stellwagen Bank National Marine Sanctuary north of Provincetown, which was

Ninety-three years after last entering New Bedford Harbor in 1921, the *Charles W. Morgan* returned on June 25, 2014. Under lower topsails with a tugboat ahead, the vessel passes through the hurricane protection barrier completed in 1966. PHOTO BY ANDY PRICE. (MYSTIC SEAPORT MUSEUM, D2014-06-0780)

When maneuvering the vessel, the first mate takes position at the bow. Here, on the anchor deck under the fore course, First Mate Sam Sikkema and Third Mate Rocky Hadler keep watch as the crew works the sails. PHOTO BY ANDY PRICE. (MYSTIC SEAPORT MUSEUM, D2014-06-1781)

"Hands to braces": the crew awaits the mate's order to haul on the starboard braces to swing the fore yards. The crew member at left keeps tension on the larboard braces with a turn around the belaying pins on the pinrail so the yards remain under control. PHOTO BY DENNIS A. MURPHY. (MYSTIC SEAPORT MUSEUM, D2014-06-0475)

A whaleboat crew launches the larboard bow boat on Stellwagen Bank in July 2014. PHOTO BY DENNIS A. MURPHY. (MYSTIC SEAPORT MUSEUM, D2014-07-1060)

Humpback whales surface near the *Morgan*'s whaleboat on Stellwagen Bank. **PHOTO BY KEN BRACEWELL. (MYSTIC SEAPORT MUSEUM, D2014-07-03)**

facilitated by the National Oceanic and Atmospheric Administration's Office of National Marine Sanctuaries. There, under sail, the *Morgan* made its way among the humpback and finback whales that frequent the bank. The Museum crew lowered the larboard bow whaleboat and rowed among the whales, which came close alongside. Here, 140 years—the sequential lifespan of two humpback whales—since killing humpbacks in the Indian Ocean, the *Morgan* sailed among them in symbolic tribute.

From Provincetown, the *Morgan* crossed Massachusetts Bay under sail and entered Boston Harbor. At the Charlestown Navy Yard, the vessel lay astern of the USS *Constitution*, the first time the oldest American naval vessel and the oldest American merchant vessel had been together.

After being celebrated in Boston, the *Morgan* sailed to the entrance of the Cape Cod Canal, then was towed back through the canal, stopping at the Massachusetts Maritime Academy for a celebration of the hundredth anniversary of the opening of the canal.

The view from the *Morgan*'s main royal yard. The coiled lines are gaskets for securing the folded and rolled sail to the yard when it is furled. (MYSTIC SEAPORT MUSEUM, D2014-09-1779)

Under full sail off New London in August 2014, the *Morgan* looks much as it did after its return to New Bedford from the West Coast in 1906. PHOTO BY DENNIS A. MURPHY. (MYSTIC SEAPORT MUSEUM, D2014-08-0770)

The *Morgan* was then towed overnight all the way back to New London. The vessel concluded its voyage with several days of cruises under sail for select Museum members and staff. Having stirred spectators wherever it went, and having taught a new generation about the intricacies of handling a square-rigged sailing vessel at sea, the *Charles W. Morgan* returned to its berth at Mystic Seaport Museum on August 6, 2014. Others will decide if it ever sails again, but what was learned and shared through the thirty-eighth voyage was priceless.

Now back at Chubb's Wharf as a museum ship—a role that has now lasted longer than the vessel's whaling career—the *Charles W. Morgan* remains an American icon, a symbol of enterprise, of bravery, of racial and ethnic collaboration in the pursuit of a goal, of the growth of the United States in the wider world. And, in its evolution from whale hunter to interpretive exhibit, the *Charles W. Morgan* helps mirror the nation's changing engagement with the natural world.

Sources and Further Reading

Ansel, Willits D., with Walter Ansel and Evelyn Ansel. *The Whaleboat: A Study of Design, Construction and Use from 1850 to 2014.* 3rd ed. Mystic, CT: Mystic Seaport Museum, 2014.

Burnett, D. Graham. *The Sounding of the Whale: Science and Cetaceans in the Twentieth Century.* Chicago: University of Chicago Press, 2013.

Busch, Briton Cooper. *Whaling Will Never Do for Me: The American Whaleman in the Nineteenth Century.* Lexington: University Press of Kentucky, 1994.

Clapham, Phil, and Colin Baxter. *Winged Leviathan: The Story of the Humpback Whale.* Grantown-on-Spey, UK: Colin Baxter Photography, 2013.

Creighton, Margaret S. *Rites and Passages: The Experience of American Whaling, 1830–1870.* Cambridge and New York: Cambridge University Press, 1995.

Davis, Lance E., Robert E. Gallman, and Karin Gleiter. *In Pursuit of Leviathan: Technology, Institutions, Productivity, and Profits in American Whaling, 1816–190*6. Chicago: University of Chicago Press, 1997.

Dolin, Eric Jay. *Leviathan: The History of Whaling in America.* New York: W. W. Norton, 2007.

Druett, Joan, ed. *"She Was a Sister Sailor": The Whaling Journals of Mary Brewster, 1845–1851.* Mystic, CT: Mystic Seaport Museum, 1992.

Ellis, Richard. *The Great Sperm Whale: A Natural History of the Ocean's Most Magnificent and Mysterious Creature.* Lawrence, KS: University Press of Kansas, 2011.

German, Andrew W., and Daniel V. McFadden. *The* Charles W. Morgan*: A Picture History of an American Icon.* Mystic, CT: Mystic Seaport Museum, 2014.

Grover, Kathryn. *Fugitive's Gibraltar: Escaping Slaves and Abolitionism in New Bedford, Massachusetts.* Amherst, MA: University of Massachusetts Press, 2001.

Haley, Nelson Cole. *Whale Hunt.* Mystic, CT: Mystic Seaport Museum, 1990.

Heflin, Wilson, edited by Mary K. Bercaw Edwards and Thomas F. Heffernan. *Herman Melville's Whaling Years.* Nashville, TN: Vanderbilt University Press, 2004.

Hohman, Elmo P. *The American Whaleman: A Study of Life and Labor in the Whaling industry.* London: Longmans, Green & Company, 1928.

Leavitt, John F. *The* Charles W. Morgan. 2nd ed. Mystic, CT: Mystic Seaport Museum, 1998.

Lund, Judith N. *Whaling Masters and Whaling Voyages from American Ports: A Compilation of Sources.* New Bedford, MA: New Bedford Whaling Museum, 2001.

Lytle, Thomas G. "Whalecraft." Whalesite.org. https://www.whalesite.org/whaling/whalecraft/index.html.

Melville, Herman, *Moby-Dick or, The Whale.* New York: Harper & Brothers, 1851; reprint, Evanston and Chicago: Northwestern University Press and The Newberry Library, 1988.

Philbrick, Nathaniel. *In the Heart of the Sea: The Tragedy of the Whaleship* Essex. New York: Viking Penguin, 2000.

Starbuck, Alexander. *History of the American Whale Fishery.* Waltham, MA: self-published, 1878; reprint, Secaucus, NJ: Castle Books, 1989.

Whaling History: Connecting All Things Whaling. Website, www.whalinghistory.org

Whitehead, Hal. *Sperm Whales: Social Evolution in the Sea.* Chicago: University of Chicago Press, 2003.

A Glossary of Whaling Terms

Ambergris. A waxy material produced in the digestive system of sperm whales in response to irritation (such as from the beaks of the giant squid they eat); ambergris is sometimes found floating at sea. Because it was an ideal stabilizer for scents in perfume, it became a very valuable occasional product for whaleships.

Bark. A sailing vessel with three or more masts, square-rigged on all but the aftermost mast, which has only fore-and-aft sails. All whaling barks were three-masted.

Barrel. A wooden cask holding about thirty-two gallons of liquid. Whalemen calculated quantities of whale oil taken in terms of 31.5-gallon barrels.

Bearers. Timbers fastened to the side of the vessel and standing upright, two between each set of davits, to steady the boats resting on the cranes, which pivot from the bearers.

Bible Leaves. The whalemen's term for the minced horse pieces of blubber, with slices cut through the fatty side, that were ready for rendering in the tryworks.

Bitter End. The inboard end of any line.

Blackfish. The whalemen's term for the pilot whale, a species of small, toothed whale. Pods of pilot whales were often encountered in the North Atlantic between New Bedford and the Azores, giving whaleboat crews a chance to practice chasing, harpooning, and lancing whales.

Blanket Piece. The strip of blubber, about six feet wide, that was cut away from the whale in a spiral pattern during the cutting-in process.

Blubber. The fatty substances that encase and insulate the body of a whale. Blubber ranges from several inches to more than a foot thick, depending upon the size and species of whale. When rendered in a whaleship's try-pots, the oil separated from the connective tissue, much as if one were frying salt pork or bacon. The process was called "trying out," or more commonly among whalemen, "boiling."

Blubber Room. The below-deck space between the crew's forecastle and the boatsteerers' and idlers' bunkrooms. This long, low room was used for cutting the large strips of blubber into smaller "horse" pieces.

Boatheader. The commander of a whaleboat. Normally, the captain headed the starboard boat, the first mate headed the larboard boat, the second mate headed the waist boat, and the third mate headed the larboard bow boat (with a fourth mate heading the starboard bow boat if carried). The boatheader steered the whaleboat during the chase and then went forward to kill the whale with a lance.

Boatsteerer. Also known as the harpooner, he pulled the forward oar in a whaleboat and had the responsibility of harpooning the whale. Once that job was done, he went aft to steer while the boatheader killed the whale with a lance.

Bomb Lance. A hollow metal projectile filled with gunpowder that was fired from a shoulder gun into a whale to explode and kill the whale. Introduced in around 1850, the bomb lance was especially useful in hunting bowhead whales, which might escape under the ice before they could be lanced by hand. The *Morgan* began carrying bomb lances in the 1850s.

Bowhead Whale. A cold-water species of baleen whale that abounds in the Bering Sea, the North Pacific, and the Sea of Okhotsk, and off the coasts of Spitzbergen and Greenland in the Atlantic. With their extremely thick blubber and long baleen, bowheads were the principal whales hunted by American whalemen from the 1840s through the 1890s.

Box. A portion of the forward deck of a whaleboat, margined at the after end by the "clumsy cleat."

Box Warp. Sometimes called the stray line, this part of the whale line was attached to the harpoon and coiled down in the "box" in the bow of the boat before passing out through the notched stem. The box warp gave the boatsteerer some slack line as he darted his harpoon.

Breakdown. As used here, it means a general get-together with music, singing, dancing, and socializing.

Bulwarks. The high, strong rail around a ship's deck.

Case. The whalemen's term for the compartment in the sperm whale's forehead that contains waxy spermaceti and may be involved in echolocation.

Clumsy Cleat. A heavy wooden brace that extends across the after end of the foredeck or box in the bow of a whaleboat. It has a notch used by the harpooner to brace his thigh as he darted his harpoon. Projecting up through it is the rod to take the forward hoisting ring or shackle. The kicking strap on its surface is knotted underneath.

Course. The lower square sail on each mast. Spoken of individually, the sail was often called by the name of the mast from which it was set. For example, the *Morgan* set a foresail and mainsail (or fore course and main course).

Cracklings. The whalemen's term for the flesh and connective tissue that remained after the oil was rendered out of the blubber. Cracklings were used to fuel the tryworks fires, producing oily, black smoke.

Cranes. Hinged, triangular wooden brackets that swing into a horizontal position from the bearers. When a whaleboat was hoisted in the davits from the water, it was set down on the cranes.

Crimps. Boardinghouse masters and agents for supplying crews in the later days of sailing ships. Crimps maintained almost complete control over crews as soon as they appeared on the waterfront.

Crosstrees. The pairs of short, horizonal spars at the points where the topmast and topgallant mast overlap and where the topgallant and royal masts overlap. The crosstrees spread the shrouds supporting the topgallant and royal mast sections and can be used as lookout platforms.

Crotch. A light, forked timber on the starboard gunwale of a whaleboat that served as a rest for the two working harpoons until they were darted.

Cutting In. The process of cutting the blubber away from the carcass of the whale as it lay in the water alongside the ship. The blubber was sectioned in a wide, spiraling blanket piece that was cut away from the musculature underneath. The vessel's mates usually performed the operation from a cutting stage rigged out over the starboard side.

Cutting Spade. A tool shaped like a spade, eight or ten inches across and sharpened along the bottom edge for cutting blubber from the whale after it was alongside the ship.

Cutting Stage. A long wooden staging, usually made up of two or three narrow planks to allow water to drain through, and extending parallel to the starboard side of the ship for about twelve feet or more. It was held out from the side of the vessel by planks extended out at right angles and suspended by tackles and lashings from the rigging and rails. Iron stanchions held a pole railing along the length of the staging, about waist high, and the mates, or those cutting in, leaned against this while wielding their cutting spades.

Cutting Tackle. Sets of double-block tackles that were hooked or shackled into a chain or rope "necklace" around the mainmast head and used for hoisting in the blubber.

Dart. The whalemen's term for the act of harpooning a whale. Harpoons could be thrown, but the preferred method was to bring the whaleboat right up to the whale so the harpoons could be driven through the blubber to anchor in the whale's flesh.

Davits. Heavy wooden timbers fastened to the sides of a whaler, two for each whaleboat; these were the unique identifying mark of whaling ships. The tops were steam-bent in a curve to form a projection. The top was slotted and fitted with sheaves or pulley wheels through which rope falls were led to form tackles for hoisting the whaleboats. The *Morgan*, as a four-boat whaler, had three pairs to larboard and one to starboard; it, as a five-boat whaler, had three to larboard and two to starboard.

Drawed. The whalemen's ungrammatical synonym for "drew." After a whale was harpooned, the harpoon sometimes pulled out and the whaleman's description was that he had "drawed his iron."

Drogue. Usually a wooden platform about 2 to 2 1/2 feet square, bridled from each corner with whale line. If a whale ran out all of the line in the tubs, the drogue was made fast to the bitter end of the second line and tossed overboard to impede the whale's progress.

Fathom. A nautical measure. One fathom equals six feet.

Finback (Fin) Whale. A species of rorqual whale that lives along the coasts and was sometimes taken by small-boat whalemen. Although common along the New England shoreline, the species was never important to the New England whaling industry.

Fluke Chain. A heavy chain that was shackled around a dead whale just forward of the flukes to secure it alongside the ship, tail forward, for cutting in.

Fluke Pipe. A hawse hole, cut low through the starboard bulwarks, through which the fluke chain was led to be attached to the fluke bitt (post) abreast of the foremast.

Footropes. Ropes strung horizontally below a ship's yards on which the crew would stand while setting or furling the square sails.

Galley or Gallied. To startle a whale and cause it to swim away before it can be harpooned. The galley is also the deck structure where all cooking is done.

Gamming. When two whaleships met at sea, if the weather was favorable, they hove to and some of the crew members visited back and forth. Gamming was very common when a captain's wife was aboard.

Goose Pen. A watertight, boxlike structure built on deck on which the brick tryworks was set. It was kept filled with water whenever there was a fire in the tryworks to prevent the deck from being scorched or set afire.

Gray Whale. A medium-size, migratory species of rorqual whale that was hunted for a time at Baja California in the 1850s, including by the *Morgan*. The females were so aggressive in protecting their calves that whalemen sometimes called them "devil fish."

Grounds. Areas in seas and oceans where whales were found to be plentiful.

Gunwale. The rail or edge of an open boat.

Harpooner. Synonymous with boatsteerer, which was the more common term in American whaleships.

Hawse Hole. An oval-shaped cut through the bulwarks of a vessel into which an iron casting is inserted and through which lines or chains are passed.

Heave Short. To take in the anchor chain by operating the windlass until the chain is vertical and the anchor is about to lift off the seabed.

Heave To (Hove To). To hold a position at sea, a ship's crew would set the wheel to steer toward the wind and the topsails to fall off the wind, thus balancing the action of the rudder so the ship remained stationary.

Hoops. Pairs of large iron rings often attached to the upper masts of whaleships to give support to the lookouts scanning the seas for spouting whales.

Horse Piece. The whalemen's term for the segments cut from the blanket piece of blubber in the blubber room. Horse pieces were about six feet long and a foot wide. They were then brought on deck to be minced into bible leaves.

Humpback Whale. A species of rorqual whale that had populations in the North and South Atlantic, around Madagascar in the Indian Ocean, and off the west coast of Central America and lower California in the Pacific. Humpbacks were fast and their carcasses often sank when killed, so they were not a major prey for New England whalers.

Iron. The whalemen's name for a harpoon.

Kanaka. The Hawaiian word for person. American whalemen used the word indiscriminately to refer to Polynesians in general and might apply it as a descriptive surname for native crew members, as in John Kanaka.

Kicking Strap. A heavy piece of line made fast at each end through holes in the "clumsy cleat" and under which the whale line passed before being coiled down in the box. The kicking strap helped control the whale line after the whale was harpooned and began to tow the whaleboat.

Knot. A measure of a ship's speed equaling one nautical mile per hour (1.15 land miles per hour). Speed was calculated with a logline, with knots spaced forty-seven feet apart, that was streamed astern for thirty seconds (measured by a sand glass). The number of knots that ran out in that time gave the number of nautical miles the vessel would travel in an hour. The *Morgan*'s 9.5-knot speed would equal just under eleven miles per hour.

Lapstrake. A form of small-boat construction where the edges of the planks are lapped one over the other and fastened at close intervals through the edges.

Larboard. A nautical term for left, especially the left side of a vessel. In the 1800s, other sea services changed to the use of "port" for left, but whalemen continued to use larboard.

Lay. Rather than receiving a set wage, whalemen were paid in the form of a share (lay) in the proceeds of the catch, less certain expenses. Lays varied from 1/15th to 1/200th, depending on the rank or experience of the men who received them, and were agreed upon as a condition of signing aboard before the voyage began.

Luff. To bring a sailing vessel up, bow into the wind, with sails shaking so that the vessel loses headway.

Nantucket Sleigh Ride. The whalemen's term for when a harpooned whale swam on the surface, towing the whaleboat at a high speed.

Right Whale. This baleen whale with thick blubber was the original species hunted in the Atlantic and remained one of the principal whales hunted by New England whalemen, who tracked them in the South Atlantic and throughout the Pacific and Indian oceans. By the 1850s, it was valued for its baleen as well as for its oil.

Rorquals. The largest group of baleen whales, including the finback, gray, humpback, and sulphur-bottom (blue) species. They are distinguished by "pleated throat grooves" that allow them to stretch their mouths greatly when feeding. Fast-swimming and prone to sinking when killed, rorquals were not widely hunted by New England whalers.

Royal. The sail above the topgallant sail, and usually the uppermost sail on any whaleship's mast.

Scrimshaw. A folk art practiced primarily by whalemen who used sperm-whale teeth, baleen (which they called whalebone), and jawbone (which they called panbone) to engrave pictures upon, or to make pie crimpers, corset busks, toys, and other articles that they took home to their wives or sweethearts. Synonyms were scrimshon and scrimshander as well as other variations of the word.

Scrimshoning. Working on scrimshaw; also written as scrimshawing or scrimshandering.

Ship. As a specific designation of rig, it means a square-rigged sailing vessel with three or more masts, all square-rigged. (Whaleships were never more than three-masted.) In generic terms, it can be used to speak of any large vessel.

Shook. The disassembled components of a cask or barrel, including staves, heads, and hoops. To save space, whaleships carried many barrels as shooks, which were reassembled by the ship's cooper as needed.

Shrouds. The term for the stays that supported the masts laterally. The tension of the stays was controlled by tightening the lanyards that ran through a pair of wooden deadeyes at the base of each stay. The shrouds were laced with horizontal ratlines to become rope ladders for the crew to go aloft.

Slide Boards. Light springy boards, about eight to ten inches wide, bent and fastened vertically to the side of the ship between the bearers or davits to hold the side of the whaleboat away and keep it from catching the gunwale on any projections as it was lowered and raised.

Slop Chest. A supply of tobacco, clothes, sheath knives, and sundries carried on board ship for the crew to purchase. The price was charged against their lay, with interest, and settled up when they were paid off at the end of the voyage. The captain usually reaped the profits.

Sound. When a whale was harpooned, it often dove and headed for the bottom. This was called sounding.

Sperm Whale. A species of toothed whale that was generally found in warmer equatorial waters but also ranged widely into both the North and South Atlantic and the Pacific. Because of the fine quality of its oil and the waxy spermaceti in its forehead "case," the sperm whale became the most desirable species for New England whalemen to hunt from the 1750s to the 1850s.

Starboard. The nautical term for right, especially the right side of a vessel. The term apparently derives from Norse-period vessels that were steered with an oar on the right, or steering side.

Stay. One of the fixed pieces of rigging that supports the masts. Originally fashioned from heavy hemp rope, after the 1860s stays were commonly made of strong but thinner wire rope. On board, stays were named for the portion of masts that they supported.

Stove. Smashed, usually by a whale. A whale would often thrash around after being harpooned or lanced and in doing so might damage or destroy the whaleboat, which would be referred to as a stove boat.

Studding Sail. A stun'sl to seamen, this lightweight sail was set outboard of a squaresail with a light-weight boom that extended outboard of the yardarm through rings. Used to increase a vessel's sail area when sailing downwind, stun'sls could be set on one or both sides of the squaresails and in varying combinations from mast to mast. Known as a fast ship, the *Morgan* carried stun'sls in her early years.

Sulphur-Bottom (Blue) Whale. A rorqual species of whale that is the largest creature on earth. Very fast and liable to sink after death, these whales are common off Antarctica and were hunted by European whalers, not New England whalemen.

Tonnage. A figure arrived at by computing a vessel's length, beam (breadth), and depth (calculated as half the breadth) in a somewhat arbitrary formula, to be used in registering or document-ing a vessel. It suggests the cargo volume of the hull but is not a measure of vessel weight or displacement.

Topgallant Mast. The third section of mast above the deck from which was set not only the topgal-lant sail but also the royal above it.

Topsail. The square sail set above the course on the section of mast above the lower mast. Begin-ning in the 1850s, the topsail was frequently divided into two sails with an extra yard or spar and became double topsails, which were easier to furl and manage in heavy winds.

Tryworks. A furnace built of bricks around two large cast-iron kettles, or try-pots, in which the blubber was rendered—tried out—to produce oil. It was positioned over the water-filled goose pen on deck aft of the fore hatch.

Waif. The whalemen's term for a small flag carried in a whaleboat that could be planted on a dead whale to claim it when several vessels were whaling in proximity.

Whale Line. Often called a tow line by whalemen, this was the line secured to the harpoon by which a whaleboat attached itself to a whale. Whale line was usually 3/4-inch long-fibered manila of the best grade. Whaleboats normally carried 1,800 feet of whale line, divided into two tubs. When breaking out a new coil, the line was led up through a temporary block aloft and down to the boatsteerer on deck to be carefully coiled into the line tub to prevent possible kinking.

Whalebone. The whalemen's term for baleen, which is actually keratin, the component of human fingernails, not bone.

Windlass. A large, horizontal, revolving timber near the bow for hoisting anchors, blanket pieces of blubber, and other heavy objects. The *Morgan* probably first had a handspike windlass, requiring the crew to turn it by hand using heavy timbers inserted in holes in the ends of the windlass barrel. The *Morgan* later had a pump-break windlass, with a long lever with a pair of handles that operated a crank mechanism. As the windlass turned, a wooden pawl dropped into notches in the center of the windlass barrel to keep it from turning backwards.

Yard. A horizontal spar to which was fastened the head or upper edge of a square sail.

Yardarm. The end of a yard.

Appendix I: *Charles W. Morgan* Logbooks and Manuscript Sources

This listing contains fifty-eight known official logbooks, abstracts, and private journals for the whaleship *Charles W. Morgan*, many of which are housed at the G. W. Blunt White Library at Mystic Seaport Museum. Periods covered vary from four days to five years.

Manuscript sources include the diaries and papers of Charles W. Morgan, the accounts of the Hillman shipyard, and assorted papers and accounts of J. & W. R. Wing and Company.

Voyage	Voyage Dates	Log Keeper (If Known)	Archive Location
1.	1841–1845	James C. Osborn	Log 52, Martha's Vineyard Historical Society
		James C. Osborn	Log 143, G. W. Blunt White Library
		Abstract	Record Group 27, National Archives and Records Administration
2.	1845–1848	Frederick Vincent	Providence Public Library
		Unknown	Log 144, G. W. Blunt White Library
		Abstract	Record Group 27, National Archives and Records Administration
3.	1849–1853	Nelson Cole Haley	Log 145, G. W. Blunt White Library
5.	1856–1859	Unknown	New Bedford Whaling Museum
6.	1859–1863	James A. Hamilton	Log 16, G. W. Blunt White Library
7.	1863–1867	Charles W. Chase	New Bedford Whaling Museum
		Charles W. Chase	Log 146, G. W. Blunt White Library
		Unknown	New Bedford Free Public Library
		Unknown	New Bedford Free Public Library
8.	1867–1871	Unknown Alvin H. Davis	Log 147, G. W. Blunt White Library Log 148, G. W. Blunt White Library
9.	1871–1874	Hiram Look	Log 409, G. W. Blunt White Library
		Unknown	New Bedford Free Public Library
10.	1875–1878	Charles L. Willis	Providence Public Library
		Unknown	New Bedford Free Public Library

11.	1878–1881	William L. Baker	KWM Log 701, New Bedford Whaling Museum
		William I. Shockley	ODHS Log 608B, New Bedford Whaling Museum
		Unknown	New Bedford Whaling Museum
12.	1881–1886	Unknown	Log 149, G. W. Blunt White Library
		Unknown	Providence Public Library
15.	1888–1889	Unknown	Log 370, G. W. Blunt White Library
17.	1890–1891	James A. M. Earle	Private Collector
18.	1891–1892	James A. M. Earle	Private Collector
19.	1892–1893	James A. M. Earle	Private Collector
20.	1893–1895	Unknown	New Bedford Free Public Library
22.	1896–1897	Antonio Margarido	Private Collector
		Unknown	Log 150, G. W. Blunt White Library
23.	1897–1898	Emanuel F. Morgan	Log 151, G. W. Blunt White Library
26.	1900–1901	Unknown	New Bedford Free Public Library
27.	1901–1902	Emanuel F. Morgan	Log 152, G. W. Blunt White Library
28.	1902–1903	Emanuel F. Morgan	G. W. Blunt White Library
		George W. Stratton	New Bedford Free Public Library
29.	1903–1904	George W. Stratton	New Bedford Free Public Library
		Unknown	New Bedford Free Public Library
30.	1904–1906	George W. Stratton	New Bedford Free Public Library
		Emanuel F. Morgan	New Bedford Free Public Library
		Discipline Log	Log 154, G. W. Blunt White Library
31.	1906–1908	Arthur O. Gibbons	Sterling Library, Yale University
		Unknown	Log 155, G. W. Blunt White Library
		Unknown	New Bedford Free Public Library
32.	1908–1910	Unknown	New Bedford Free Public Library
		Charlotte Church	Log 156, G. W. Blunt White Library
33.	1911–1913	William H. Griffiths	Log 157, G. W. Blunt White Library
		William H. Griffiths	Log 158, G. W. Blunt White Library
		William H. Griffiths	G. W. Blunt White Library
		Unknown	Barbara Johnson Collection
		Unknown	KWM Log 501 v1, New Bedford Whaling Museum
		Unknown	New Bedford Free Public Library
34.	1916–1917	Benjamin D. Cleveland	G. W. Blunt White Library
		John D. Lopes	Log 159, G. W. Blunt White Library

35.	1918–1919	Unknown	New Bedford Whaling Museum
		Unknown	Log 160, G. W. Blunt White Library
36.	1919–1920	John F. Edwards	KWM, New Bedford Whaling Museum
37.	1920–1921	Unknown	New Bedford Whaling Museum
		Unknown	Log 161, G. W. Blunt White Library

MANUSCRIPT SOURCES

Account of Payments for Labor on New Ship Building for C. W. Morgan by J. & Z. Hillman, VFM 1744, G. W. Blunt White Library

Accounts of Sperm and Right Whales Seen, KWM A-173, New Bedford Whaling Museum

Bill of Sale, *Charles W. Morgan*, 1841–1852, VFM 1752, G. W. Blunt White Library

Charles W. Morgan Collection, Coll. 27, G. W. Blunt White Library

Charles W. Morgan, Diaries, Coll. 27, vols. 1–43, G. W. Blunt White Library

Charles W. Morgan, Papers and Correspondence, 1831–1911, VFM 1770, G. W. Blunt White Library

Charles W. Morgan, Accounts, Settlement of Crew, Bill of Sale, 1863–1899, KWM Mss Coll., Box 5, Folder 1, New Bedford Whaling Museum

Charles W. Morgan, Crew Lists (copies of originals at National Archives and Records Administration), G. W. Blunt White Library

Hillman Shipyard Collection, 1827–1862, Collection 9, G. W. Blunt White Library

J. & W. R. Wing and Company, Papers and Accounts, New Bedford Free Public Library

J. & W. R. Wing and Company, Papers and Accounts, New Bedford Whaling Museum

Appendix II: Summary of Voyages of the *Charles W. Morgan*

The following summary of voyages and gross value of cargoes was compiled from information bulletins compiled by Dr. Charles R. Schultz and members of the staff of the G. W. Blunt White Library at Mystic Seaport Museum, with reference to the account books of Charles W. Morgan in the G. W. Blunt White Library and to the business records of J. & W. R. Wing and Company in the New Bedford Free Public Library, available on microfilm at the New Bedford Whaling Museum.

Voyage #1.	Sailed from New Bedford, September 6, 1841
	Thomas A. Norton, Master; Charles W. Morgan et al., owners
	Returned to New Bedford, January 1, 1845
	Value of cargo, $53,052.56
Voyage #2.	Sailed from New Bedford, June 10, 1845
	John D. Samson, Master; Charles W. Morgan et al., owners
	Returned to New Bedford, December 9, 1848
	Value of cargo, $75,011.09
Voyage #3.	Sailed from New Bedford, June 5, 1849
	John D. Samson, Master; Edward M. Robinson et al., owners
	Returned to New Bedford, May 27, 1853
	Value of cargo, $44,138.75
Voyage #4.	Sailed from New Bedford, September 20, 1853
	Tristam P. Ripley, Master; I. Howland Jr. & Company, agents
	Returned to New Bedford, April 27, 1856
	Value of cargo, $76,183.64
Voyage #5.	Sailed from New Bedford, September 15, 1856
	Thomas N. Fisher, Master; I. Howland Jr. & Company, agents
	Returned to New Bedford, April 16, 1859
	Value of cargo, $62,720.84
Voyage #6.	Sailed from New Bedford, October 4, 1859
	James A. Hamilton, Master; I. Howland Jr. & Company, agents
	Returned to New Bedford, May 12, 1863
	Value of cargo, $165,405.74

Voyage #7.	Sailed from New Bedford, December 1, 1863
	Thomas C. Landers, Master; J. & W. R. Wing, owners
	Returned to New Bedford, June 12, 1867
	Value of cargo, $58,125.16
	1,286 days; average $45.19 per day
Voyage #8.	Now rerigged as a bark and remeasured to register 313.75 tons
	Sailed from New Bedford, July 17, 1867
	George Athearn, Master; J. & W. R. Wing, owners
	Returned to New Bedford, August 16, 1871
	Value of cargo, $54,975.52
	1,491 days; average $36.27 per day
Voyage #9.	Sailed from New Bedford, September 26, 1871
	John M. Tinkham, Master; J. & W. R. Wing, owners
	Returned to New Bedford, October 31, 1874
	Value of cargo, $69,060.59
	1,132 days; average $64.27 per day
Voyage #10.	Sailed from New Bedford, April 23, 1875
	John M. Tinkham, Master; J. & W. R. Wing, owners
	Returned to New Bedford, May 17, 1878
	Value of cargo, $31,869.00
	1,119 days; average $28.21 per day
Voyage #11.	Sailed from New Bedford, July 17, 1878
	Thomas L. Ellis, Master; J. & W. R. Wing, owners
	Returned to New Bedford, May 11, 1881
	Value of cargo, $47,588.59
	1,028 days; average $46.29 per day
Voyage #12.	Sailed from New Bedford, July 13, 1881
	Charles F. Keith, Master; J. & W. R. Wing, owners
	Returned to New Bedford, June 18, 1886
	Value of cargo, $46,693.34
	1,801 days; average $25.17 per day
Voyage #13.	Sailed from New Bedford, October 6, 1886
	George A. Smith, Master; J. & W. R. Wing, owners
	Returned to San Francisco, November 4, 1887
	Value of cargo, $33,645.70
Voyage #14.	Sailed from San Francisco, December 3, 1887
	George A. Smith, Master; J. & W. R. Wing, owners
	Returned to San Francisco, November 5, 1888
	Value of cargo, $20,327.21

Voyage #15.	Sailed from San Francisco, November 26, 1888
	John S. Layton, Master; J. & W. R. Wing, owners
	Returned to San Francisco, October 27, 1889
	Value of cargo, $23,752.49
Voyage #16.	Sailed from San Francisco, December 5, 1889
	John S. Layton, Master; J. & W. R. Wing, owners
	Returned to San Francisco, November 8, 1890
	Value of cargo, $13,725.20
Voyage #17.	Sailed from San Francisco, December 2, 1890
	James A. M. Earle, Master; J. & W. R. Wing, owners
	Returned to San Francisco, October 31, 1891
	Value of cargo, $29,669.49
Voyage #18.	Sailed from San Francisco, November 24, 1891
	James A. M. Earle, Master; J. & W. R. Wing, owners
	Returned to San Francisco, November 7, 1892
	Value of cargo, $10,643.97
Voyage #19.	Sailed from San Francisco, December 8, 1892
	James A. M. Earle, Master; J. & W. R. Wing, owners
	Returned to San Francisco, November 9, 1893
	Value of cargo, $10,949.16
Voyage #20.	Sailed from San Francisco, December 6, 1893
	James A. M. Earle, Master; J. & W. R. Wing, owners
	Returned to San Francisco, November 5, 1895
	Value of cargo, $47,270.80
Voyage #21.	Sailed from San Francisco, December 2, 1895
	James A. M. Earle, Master; J. & W. R. Wing, owners
	Returned to San Francisco, November 1, 1896
	Value of cargo, $14,197.70
Voyage #22.	Sailed from San Francisco, December 3, 1896
	John S. Layton, Master; J. & W. R. Wing, owners
	Returned to San Francisco, October 25, 1897
	Value of cargo, $22,610.65
Voyage #23.	Sailed from San Francisco, November 11, 1897
	Thomas Scullun, Master; J. & W. R. Wing, owners
	Returned to San Francisco, October 28, 1898
	Value of cargo, $18,075.48

Voyage #24.	Sailed from San Francisco, November 26, 1898
	Thomas Scullun, Master; J. & W. R. Wing, owners
	Returned to San Francisco, November 2, 1899
	Value of cargo, $20,149.95
Voyage #25.	Sailed from San Francisco, December 7, 1899
	Thomas Scullun, Master; J. & W. R. Wing, owners
	Returned to San Francisco, October 29, 1900
	Value of cargo, $17,684.73
Voyage #26.	Sailed from San Francisco, November 22, 1900
	James A. M. Earle, Master; J. & W. R. Wing, owners
	Returned to San Francisco, October 29, 1901
	Value of cargo, $38,565.94
Voyage #27.	Sailed from San Francisco, November 27, 1901
	Thomas Scullun, Master; J. & W. R. Wing, owners
	Returned to San Francisco, October 28, 1902
	Value of cargo, $34,289.83
Voyage #28.	Sailed from San Francisco, November 20, 1902
	James A. M. Earle, Master; J. & W. R. Wing, owners
	Returned to San Francisco, October 27, 1903
	Value of cargo, $26,614.51
Voyage #29.	Sailed from San Francisco, November 18, 1903
	James A. M. Earle, Master; J. & W. R. Wing, owners
	Returned to San Francisco, October 31, 1904
	Value of cargo, $26,318.52
	347 days; average $62.98 per day
Voyage #30.	Sailed from San Francisco, November 25, 1904
	Edwin J. Reed, Master; J. & W. R. Wing, owners
	Returned to New Bedford, June 12, 1906
	Value of cargo, $20,294.36
	564 days; average $35.94 per day
Voyage #31.	Sailed from New Bedford, August 11, 1906
	James A. M. Earle, Master, succeeded by Captain Hiram Nye; J. & W. R. Wing, owners
	Returned to New Bedford, July 4, 1908
	Value of cargo, $34,081.62

Voyage #32.	Sailed from New Bedford, September 2, 1908
	Arthur O. Gibbons, Master, succeeded by Captain Charles S. Church; J. & W. R. Wing, owners
	Returned to New Bedford, September 12, 1910
	Value of cargo, $34,271.69
	740 days; average $46.31 per day
Voyage #33.	Sailed from New Bedford, May 10, 1911
	Charles S. Church, Master; J. & W. R. Wing, owners
	Returned to New Bedford, August 9, 1913
	Value of cargo, $39,748.94
	821 days; average $48.41 per day
Voyage #34.	Sailed from New Bedford, September 5, 1916
	Benjamin D. Cleveland, Master and owner
	Returned to New Bedford, October 23, 1917
	Value of cargo, $21,766.50
Voyage #35.	Sailed from New Bedford, July 16, 1918 (hailing from Provincetown)
	Joseph D. Edwards, Master; John A. Cook, owner
	Returned to New Bedford, September 7, 1919
	Value of cargo, $26,444.25
Voyage #36.	Sailed from New Bedford, October 18, 1919
	Joseph F. Edwards, Master and part owner
	Returned to New Bedford, July 16, 1920
	Value of cargo $8,977.50
Voyage #37.	Sailed from New Bedford, September 9, 1920
	John Gonsalves, Master; J. A. Cook, owner
	Returned to Provincetown, May 28, 1921, then to New Bedford
	Value of cargo, $25,533.90

Appendix III: *Charles W. Morgan* Crew Lists

Listed below are the crew members of the *Charles W. Morgan* throughout its whaling career of thirty-seven recorded voyages from September 6, 1841, through September 9, 1920. The list is complete insofar as records presently known allow. The bulk of her crew members was obtained from the vessel's official crew lists on file in the National Archives and Records Administration and from the J. & W. R. Wing and Company account books, which cover the *Morgan*'s voyages from December 1, 1863, through August 9, 1913. Where possible, the names were cross-checked among all four of the sources for this compilation: official customhouse records of the vessel, where extant; Charles W. Morgan's business records; New Bedford's whaling newspaper, the *Whalemen's Shipping List*; and the Wing account books. In some cases, only the names of the crew that shipped for the initial leg of the voyage were available. Subsequent shipping, discharging, and desertion records are sometimes incomplete, depending on the voyage. Asterisks indicate those who were aboard for the entire voyage.

This compilation is not clear cut, since names were frequently spelled in two or three ways, due to the illiteracy of many of the men or the whim of the officers or agents who signed them. Such is particularly the case with Japanese sailors, who received a phonetic approximation of their name, and of Polynesian sailors, who might be named for their islands or be given Anglo-Saxon names by the officers. Furthermore, people would often change their names when shipping if they were going to sea to get away from home or escape the law. In the case of a conflict in spelling, the official government records were taken in preference to any other. In cases of questionable legibility, the most legible, if not in conflict with official records, was taken. Yet, some names remain a puzzle, an example being "Luis Gamatuatan," a native of Guam, who sailed three times from 1891 to 1896, with a different spelling each time. Indeed, his name may properly have been Luis G. Manotanto, as it was listed on one occasion!

In a number of cases, a unified spelling has been adopted for what is clearly the same name spelled different ways in succeeding voyages, especially when age, residence, and physical description match. Unfortunately, time and incomplete records did not allow for full checking. The long careers of John E. D. Smith and George P. Christian are two examples that are believed to be correct but need further checking to substantiate fully.

The original list was compiled with the assistance of the National Archives and Records Administration and Reginald B. Hegarty of the New Bedford Free Public Library.

CREW LISTS
VOYAGE 1 (SEPTEMBER 6, 1841–JANUARY 1, 1845)

*Thomas A. Norton, Master
Charles S. Chadwick, 1st Mate, discharged at Paita
*James C. Osborn, 2nd Mate
*William A. Look, 3rd Mate
*Allen M. Athearn
Orlando Blake
Thomas K. Coffin
*William H. Coffin
*James Connelly
Thomas Curtis
Henry Johnson Dally Domingo
*William Dunham
*Samuel O. Fisher
*Zenas Gould
William Harris Hector
*Samuel J. Hudson
Holmes Jernegan
*Nathan M. Jernegan
*Miles A. Johnson
Thomas Kanaka
*Manuel Lopez
*John A. Luce
Barney McGee
*Stillman Manter
*Timothy Mayhew
George Morgan
Vicente Muscoso
*William R. Norton
*William Osborn
George Porter
Samuel Robinson
Charles Scriber
Isaac C. Smith
*Philander Smith
*Manuel Tavares
Jacob Thompson
*Abraham Weaver

VOYAGE 2 (JUNE 10, 1845–DECEMBER 9, 1848)

*John D. Samson, Master
*William W. Clement, 1st Mate
*Frederick Vincent, 2nd Mate
*William Griffin, 3rd Mate
*John Antone
Diego Aquisa
John Barker
Samuel Benedict
William Black
Robert Bolton
*Amos Brown
W. H. Brownell
Henry J. Coop
Robert Cox
John Craig
Charles Cushman (died)
*John Doramus
Henry Ferrara
Joe Ferrera
William Firth
J. Frank
John Friday
*Zenas Gould
Thomas Hardy
William H. Herbert
*Enoch Hookway
William Hundray
Josiah Hutchinson
William A. Johnson
*John Lattick
Henry A. Lincoln
*Antone F. Mayo
William McLane
*William McLoughlin
George Morgan
Dick Morris
Levi Otaheite
Thomas W. Owens
*Thacher Packard
Ben Rotch
John E. Stafford
*James Tate
*Henry Tilley
Levi Tobey
William Town
Diego Vasquez
Isaac Walton
Abraham H. Weaver
Henry White
*James D. Whiteside

VOYAGE 3 (JUNE 5, 1849–MAY 27, 1853)

*John D. Samson, Master
*Thacher Packard, 1st Mate
*William Griffin, 2nd Mate
*Roland Briggs, 3rd Mate
John Adams
*William Auza
*Stephen Barnum
John Barker
*Benjamin Butman
Amasa Colby
*William L. Covell
*Charles Coy
Vincent D. Crowl
Lewis Dorr
*George Duffy
Enos Eastwood
*Moses F. Gardner
*Mathew Gilgannon
*Nelson C. Haley
Joseph Maxwell
*Benjamin Olney
James W. Parker
*Thomas Phillips
Ben Rotch
Thomas Ryan
*Daniel W Sampson
*Thomas A. Tyler Jr.
*Smith Tucker
David Van Riper
Francis Warner
Martin Whitehead
*Joseph Whitman

VOYAGE 4 (SEPTEMBER 20, 1853–APRIL 27, 1856)

*Tristram P. Ripley, Master
Stephen Devoll, 1st Mate, discharged at Lahaina
*Ariel Norton, 2nd Mate
*Joseph C. Airey
*Manuel Alexander
Antone Bemamona
James Boyd
*William Corey
David E. Dean
William Denzmore
*Alvin H. Davis
*Samuel F. Davis
John Druse
*John Erwin
J. P. Fisher
*Samuel H. Haines
William Hall
Hawanui
Charles Jackson
Kaavea
Kaulahea
*Antone Lewis
John Macey
*Thomas Malone
Joe Manuel
Keav Nin
*Charles E. Phelps
Jacinth Pray
*John Read
*John Riccols
*Benjamin Ripley
*Justus J. Sampson
*Whitcomb Sampson
*Frederick Snadaker
*John M. Tucker
*George F. Winslow

VOYAGE 5 (SEPTEMBER 15, 1856–APRIL 16, 1859)

*Thomas N. Fisher, Master
*Thomas W. Johnson, 1st Mate
*Samuel F. Davis, 2nd Mate
*David Carrington, 3rd Mate
*Charles W. Addams
Eugene H. Anderson
Friday Ascension
Joe Ascension
Tom Ascension

James O. Brian
Franco Brooks
*John Cabit
William G. Crowell
*John R. Cuff
Charles D. Daggett
Manuel Deos
William H. Drew
James H. Evans
*Henry Francis
*Peter Galena
*James Hamlin
James Harrison

*Edward Hobbs
Charles G. Kline
George M. Lam
Edward LeBaron
George McLean
*William B. Marchant
*Antonio Medeiros
*Jose Miguel
*Joseph N. Mill
*Albert Palmer
*Edward L. Pangburn
*Michael Pease
Charles Pitts

John Raphael
*Dickenson Read
*John Reed
*Alexander Reyot
William Robinson
Joseph Roderiguez
George Ross
Smith Rowland
Antonio Sabina
*Edwin Sleight
*Antone Sylvia
Lewis Verra
*William Young

VOYAGE 6 (OCTOBER 4, 1859–MAY 12, 1863)

*James A. Hamilton, Master
*George Smith, 1st Mate
*John Williams, 2nd Mate
*Peter Sylvia, 3rd Mate
Daniel Andrews
David Baker
Martin Barrett
David Beaton
Lewis Becker
*Ansel E. Braley
Truman B. Braley
Thomas Brown
Rodney S. Campbell
Henry Carter
Joe Carter
Charles
Henry Clay
Manuel da Rose Coello
J. J. Coleman
Charles Crim
Robert Darling
John H. Dattin
Charles Davis
Jose de Canto
Jose del la Costa
Ceracio de la Rosa
Joseph N. de Malo
Dick

John Dyer
Henry Eldridge
Joe
John Enos
George Faville
Peter Fernandez
Barney Fisher
Joseph Fisher
Frank
Henry Hillman
Jarvis G. Horton
Juan N. Janos
William B. Johnson
Kaluna Keahu
Kealoha
Julian Knowles
John H. Lathrop
Thomas F. Laycock (drowned)
Nicholas Gabrino
George Gibson
George W Gifford
Antonio Gonzales
Silvanus S. Gove
John Grady
Richard Griswold
Horace O. Hancock
Liman G. Hensted
Alonzo Levally

Antone Lopez
Louis
Anton Ludwig
Francis McEvena
John McIntyre
James McTier
Richard H. Mead
John Martin
Harry Mokii
Edward Ormesby
Asa Page
John Perano
Frank Perry
Peter
Thomas Philbrook
Andrew J. Phillips
James Phillips
John Pleasant
Daniel Quinn
Elijah Rathbone
Samuel N. Richardson
Riley
William Roach
John Roche
Antone Roderick
Manuel Roderick
Bill Rotuman
Bob Rotuman
Frank Rotuman

Friday Rotuman
Jack Rotuman
Peter Rotuman
Manuel Saldinia
Thomas Sherman
William H. Shippen
Antonio Silvia
Peter Silvia
William Slater
Charles Smith
George Smith
Charles Solano
Jose Tenelasco
John Thompson
Guillermo Torres
James A. Tripp
Francisco Ulloa
Alex Upham
Robert S. Valentine
James Wallace
Thomas C. Webb
William
William Whitelaw
John Williams
James Wilson
James S. Wise
John Wright

(Lack of original records prevents full identification of those who completed voyage 6)

VOYAGE 7 (DECEMBER 1, 1863–JUNE 12, 1867)

*Thomas C. Landers, Master
*Charles W. Chace, 1st Mate

*William Harlow, 2nd Mate
*Benjamin White, 3rd Mate
Albion

*Charles Amory
Amos
William P. Anderson
*William F. Benton
Cashman

*Antone Christ
*Daniel Connus
*John Crowley
*William Curran
*Manuel Francis

Frank	Johnson	Minor	John Smith
*Elijah Fuller	*John Jose	Allen Nye	*Bartholomew Sullivan
*John Gardner	Kelly	*Edward Parrott	William Taylor
Goemes	*A. H. Lambert	Manuel Penas	Tom
*Antone L. Gonsalves	Arthur L. Landers	Felix Reno	*Oliver P. Tufts
Goodyear	(drowned)	James R. Royce	Wilder
*William Gorman	Little	Joseph Silva	*James Williams
Horn	Nagindo Marinda	Abner Simmons	Wilson

(Lack of original records prevents full identification of the crew of voyage 7)

VOYAGE 8 (JULY 17, 1867–AUGUST 16, 1871)

*George Athearn, Master	Joseph Brown	John Grob	Thomas Nesmith
Alvin H. Davis, 1st Mate (died)	Albert N. Butts	William Handy	Jules Nicholas
	Joseph Carvo	Oswald Julp	John Orrotanga
*Frederick C. Swain, 2nd Mate	William L. G. Chace	Jack Kanaka	Ben Resanta
	*Jerome Chochin	Moa Kanaka	*John Silva
*Frank Roderick, 3rd Mate	Santa de Croze	*Fred LeBaron	George Schlick (died)
	*Antone M. de Suza	Antone Lewis	George H. Smith
*Edwin W. Athearn, 4th Mate	Antone Dolires	Enas Lewis	John E. D. Smith
	*Manuel Dundrade	*Hiram W. Look	Lewis Smith
Antone Aenas	William H. Fish	William McHenry	Levi Swift
Megil Agosta	Jack Fisher	James C. McKeever	Manuel Thomas
John Andrews	Phillip Folpe	Jim Mangra	J. E. Waterbury
*Matthais Antonio	Francisco Foster	Joking Michael	Ishmael White
Joseph Barre	Antonio Francisco	William Monroe	Bob Whytootake
August Bottzer	*Anthony J. Frates	G. H. Myers	
Charles M. Brown	John Frates	*Antone Nesmit	

VOYAGE 9 (SEPTEMBER 26, 1871–OCTOBER 31, 1874)

*John M. Tinkham, Master	Theodore L. Bennett (drowned)	James D. Kinzer	Joseph Monzairs
		Joseph King	Thomas Morgan
*Wanton S. Beauvais, 1st Mate	William Charles	Merdene Kiouse	Patrick O'Brien
	*Leonte D. Cross	August Kornumpsky	*Manuel J. Perry
Andrew Jackson, 2nd Mate	Alcide Dart	F. Lamb	Philip Rozette
	Frank Deas	Joseph Leamon	*Louis M. Santo
*Frank Roderick, 3rd Mate	*Joseph De Lumbo	Antone M. Lemos	*William Schmidt
	*Jose de Simos	Mohee Lewis	*Richard Settle
Antone Nesmith, 4th Mate	Manuel de Souza	*Hiram W. Look	John Sharpe
	Bud O. Fees	Domingo Lopez	Henry Smith
Charles Adams	John Flynn	August Macoxa	*John E. D. Smith
Amille Adlos	*Manuel Francis	Joe Martin	*Mariano J. Souares
St. Cyr. Adolphe	Lewis Gonsalves	A. Meail	Charles Theuile
Nemoine Anacos	Joseph Hall	*Herman Meinhardt	*Antonio Vieria
Enos Avilla	Marbois Henry	Jacob Meinhardt	John M. Vincent
Howard Beaumont	Alphonses James	*John Miller	*John Williams
	Philo M. Joan	*Pliney Mitchell	Peter Zette

VOYAGE 10 (APRIL 23, 1875–MAY 17, 1878)

*John M. Tinkham, Master	*Charles L. Willis, 3rd Mate	Fernando Aviera	C. Wells Coggeshall
		Epolito Bernado	Willie F. Cook
*Daniel L. Ricketson, 1st Mate	*Eanos D. Avilla, 4th Mate	*Manuel Bravo	Jose Cuemintel
		William Brown	Manuel da Costa
Antonio Silva, 2nd Mate	Meguil Alvez	Francisco Cabral	Jose da Freitas
	Jose Antone	Manuel Cabral	Turibio da Lomba

Manuel da Rosa
Marcellino da Silva
Jerome DeFrates
Megil Delgardo
Francisco de Souza
Jose de Mello
Carlos de Penna (died)
Jose de Soito
Charles Dowdell
Aaron W. Drew
Julio Duarte
Edward J. Dyer

Eugene W. Fish
Martin Flood
J. J. Fonseca
Manuel Fustino
Joseph Hall
Andrew Harrison
Adolphus Hayard
Albert N. Haskins
Frank Howell
Antonio Jacinto
John Jack
Andrew Jackson

Joseph King
John Knipe
Antonio Lego
Manuel Lopes
George T. Marshall
Jose A. Martino
Pedro Miller
Jose Monteira
Charles O. Morse
Antone Penaro
Irving A. Perry
Joseph S. Perry

*Charles M. Sanborn
Fred Schneickhardt
Joao J. Senna
Albert Silva
Joao Simoes
*John E. D. Smith
George J. Thomas
Thomas H. Turner
Dixie C. Twombly
Antone Vera
Charles A. Wood
Joseph Young

VOYAGE 11 (JULY 17, 1878–MAY 11, 1881)

*Thomas L. Ellis, Master
*John B. Tobey, 1st Mate
*Joseph King, 2nd Mate
*William I. Shockley, 3rd
    Mate
Sabine Alps
*Megel Antone
*Manuel Arenas
*Ferdinand Avery
*Joseph A. Bailey
*William L. Baker
Samuel Brooks
Thomas Brown
*Charles F. Coleman
Antone Corea

*Manuel Coreia
James Crow
Manuel da Costa
Henrique de Brit
Jose D. de Lemos
Rufus de Ramos
*Manuel de Roza
Jose de Silvia
John Eanos
*Arthur C. Eldridge
John Ellis
Antone Fillis
*William C. Fish
*Joseph L. Fortes
Casimere Gonsalves

*Nicholas Gonsalves
*Manuel Gracia
*John Harding
*Albert N. Haskins
*Manuel Jackson
*Oren B. Jeffers
*Peter Johnson
William Johnson
Antone Lopez
*Charles S. Manchester
Jose Marks
*Joseph Mendoze
Manuel Mitchell
Bernardo Prariea
*Antonio Rezende

*Charles Sanborn
Antone Santa
*John E. D. Smith
Jones Smith
*Joseph Sylva
Isaac Sylvia
Joseph S. Sylvia
Manuel Sylvia
Albert Thomas
*Joseph Thomas
*William W. White
*Rudolphus L. Wordell

VOYAGE 12 (JULY 13, 1881–JUNE 17, 1886)

*Charles F. Keith, Master
*James F. Lawrence, 1st
    Mate
*Joseph King, 2nd Mate
*Peter John, 3rd Mate
James S. Howland, 4th
    Mate (drowned)
George Allibaw
Frank Alpheus
*Henry J. Clarke
*Jose Correa
Lawrence Correa

Robert W. Craig (died)
*Manuel P. Delgado
*Goddance de Pena
Phileme de Silvia
Antone Edwards
Charles Fisher
*Henry Gelkes
Jose A. Gomez
*Casimere Gonsalves
*George Groth
John Harding
*George Hassell

*Augustus E. Hawkes
Max Herman
*William B. Keith
Antone Lopez
Jose Lopez
*Douglass McDonald
*N. A. Martin
*Jose Morano
Marcellino Morea
William H. Morey
Ernest Mountain
Jose Ramos

Earl C. Russell (died)
*Ernest Secara
Enos Seckava
*Lewis V Semedo
Frederick Seymore
*John A. Simmons
*John E. D. Smith
James Wallace
John Wallis
*Thomas Waters
Harry Wilson
George E. Yale

VOYAGE 13 (OCTOBER 6, 1886–NOVEMBER 4, 1887)

*George A. Smith, Master
*John S. Layton, 1st Mate
*William F. Allen, 2nd
    Mate
*Andrew T. Nash, 3rd
    Mate
*Ensign E. Baker, 4th
    Mate
*John Allen
*Lewis G. Andrews

*James Antone
*Edward Arnold
Joseph Bement
*Joseph F. Branch
*Charles Brines
*George Brown
George Cody
*Crispolo de Aris
*Antonio F. de Grass
Jose de Los Santos

*Manuel P. Delgado
*John Frara
*William J. George
Bartholomew F. Gomez
G. Hirrera
*Henry W. Howland
*Orlando M. Lumbert
*Joseph Lewis
*Clement Lopez
*Willie McCormick

*William McKutchinson
*Honorio A. Martin
William J. Mitchell
Juan Quitagua
*Thomas Pena
Fred W. Robinson
*Marcellino Rose
*Otto Schuler
Jose Sequina
*John E. D. Smith

VOYAGE 14 (DECEMBER 3, 1887–NOVEMBER 5, 1888)

*George A. Smith, Master
*Silvanus C. Waldron, 1st Mate
*John H. Gifford, 2nd Mate
*Henry Rodrigues, 3rd Mate
*Honorio A. Martin, 4th Mate
*John Andrus
Jim Antone (drowned)
*George Brown
*Leander G. Cobb
*Dominico de Costa
*Manuel de la Rosa
*Manuel F. de Limas
*August Engstrom
*Ben Fausto
*William J. George
*Antone Joseph
James Kennett
*Jim Kanaka
*C. Kurz
*Jacob Lena
*John McBride
*William McKutchinson
*Edward Maillot
*James Marshall
*Frank Mitchell
*Manuel Morgan
*Phillip Montes
S. R. Pickersgill (drowned)
*Pat Power
*Joe Santos
*Joe Sirvance
*Charles Stanton
*Jose Titano
W. W. Whiting
George Williams (died)
*Edward J. Wilson

VOYAGE 15 (NOVEMBER 26, 1888–OCTOBER 27, 1889)

*John S. Layton, Master
*Andrew D. West, 1st Mate
*A. Spiering, 2nd Mate
*Antone Cabral, 3rd Mate
*Honorio A. Martin, 4th Mate
Charles Alberts
*Carl Baptista
John Ball
*George Brown
James Cole
*G. W. Conover
*John M. Cornell Jr.
Charles Edwards
*Manuel F. de Limas
Ben Fausto
*Emidio Fernandes
*John Frazer
*W. H. Freeman
*William J. George
Aleck Kanaka (died)
Dick Kanaka (died)
Harry Kanaka
Pray Kanaka
*Jack Kelley
*Henry M. King
Fred Lucas
*Wilham McKutchinson
*Edward Maillot
*James Marshall
Antone Merry
*William J. Morris
Teoprice Oporgydobe Partill
*George H. Peckham
*Stephen Pena
*John F. Perry
Pat Power
*John Sablan
*Joe Santos
*Charles Smith
Chalmers Smyth
*Charles Stanton
*Jose Taitano
*George W. Topping
*Edmund Verbracken
*Joseph Vincent
Wagner

VOYAGE 16 (DECEMBER 5, 1889–NOVEMBER 8, 1890)

*John S. Layton, Master
*William F. Allen, 1st Mate
Honorio A. Martin, 2nd Mate
*Antone Cabral, 3rd Mate
*Simeon C. Leach, 4th Mate
*Adoniram J. Jones, 5th Mate
*John Branscombe
*Fred Brown
*George Brown
*Ben Castro
J. B. Cook
*John M. Cornell Jr.
Emidio Fernandes
*Theodore Florence
William H. Griffith
B. F. Hargrave
*Otto Hartman
Jacob Jones
*Jack Kelley
Harry A. Kluge
*Joaquim Lopes
William Madigan
*Edward Maillot
*William J. Morris
*A. Nyberg
*Henry Orchatz
John Peters
*Ignacious Sablan
John Saipan
Antone Santos
Felice Selihan
*Joe Sequin
Antone Silva
*Charles Smith
*John E. D. Smith
*William Smith
*Charles Stanton
Tom Stephensen
G. W. Taylor
*Edmund Verbracken
Domingo Blas
Enos Chaco

(Harry Bram, shipping master, reports that Blas and Chaco signed for the bark *Cape Horn Pigeon* but went by mistake on *Charles W. Morgan*. As a result, neither man was paid his advance of $50 since it was not known that they were aboard.)

VOYAGE 17 (DECEMBER 2, 1890–OCTOBER 31, 1891)

*James A. M. Earle, Master
*Daniel W. Gifford, 1st Mate
*William W. James, 2nd Mate
*Simeon C. Leach, 3rd Mate
*Jose de Gloria, 4th Mate
*Frank Bauer
Domingo Blas
*John Branscombe
*George Brown
*Ben Castro
Enos Chaco (died)
*Enos de la Crus
Ignacia de la Cruz
J. De La Cruze
Vicente de la Cruze
Jose de San Nicholas
John Driver
Bernabe Enecenio
*Robert N. Flanders
*Charles S. Hait
*August Heinemann
*Edward Johnson
*Peter Johnson
*William Madigan
Charles Marston
*Felix Martinez
Nicholas Matigan
*N. Matsutara

Charles Meyers
Peter Peres
*Charles Peterson
Vicenti Quantanilla
Joaquim Quinatta

*Ysidorio Ramos
*Celo Regis
*John Roberts
*Joseph Rodgers
*Manuel Rose

*Vicento Rose
*John S. Ross
*Felix Sablan
*Joseph Sablan
Jose Santos

*Joe Sequinda
*Hermann Smith
*John E. D. Smith
Charles Stanton
*Nelson Wilson

VOYAGE 18 (NOVEMBER 24, 1891–NOVEMBER 7, 1892)

*James A. M. Earle, Master
Robert N. Flanders, 1st Mate
*William W. James, 2nd Mate
*Frank Enos, 3rd Mate
*Charles A. Howland, 4th Mate
*Frank Bauer, 5th Mate
Tilge Aflague
*Peder Andersen

*Carl Baptista
*Jose Benchimol
*Domingo Blas
*John Branscombe
*George Brown
*Lucas Castro
*Leander G. Cobb
*Jose de Castro
*Saberin Diaz
*E. Doneburgh
Antone Gorman
*Thomas James

*Joaquim Karado
*Jack Kelley
*Harry A. Kluge
*Charles F. Koch
*Ben Longrero
*Felix Martines
*Ramon Mesa
*Andrew Meyer
*Nicholas Malaia
*Peter Peres
Ysidorio Ramos
Fred Richter

*Ben Rose
*John S. Ross
*Joseph Sablan
*Joe Silva
*Seraphine Silva
John Stephens
*W. H. Summers
James Walker
*Charles Winters

VOYAGE 19 (DECEMBER 8, 1892–NOVEMBER 9, 1893)

*James A. M. Earle, Master
*Horace F. Tower, 1st Mate
*Frank Enos, 2nd Mate
*George H. Peckham, 3rd Mate
*Felix Aflague
*Peder Andersen
*Carl Baptista
*Frank Bauer
*Jose Benchimol
*John Branscombe
*George Brown

*Otto Carl
*Richard Carter
*Lucas Castro
*Jose de Castro
Manuel de la Concepcion
Juan de la Cruze
Nicholas de Salas
*Peter Feeney
Anselmo Glacioas
*William A. Goering
*Antone Gomes
*John Gomes
Louis Gamatuatan
*Thomas James

*William W. James
*John Jacobs
Henry Johnson
*Sam Kahaunaele
*William Kailiuli
*Joaquim Karado
*Jack Kelley
*Harry A. Kluge
*Charles F Koch
*Vicento Longrero
*Peter Lopez
*John Lin
*William McDonald
*Samuel McIntyre

*Joe Manalisea
*Nicholas Malaia
*Jose Nego
*Charles Petroesch
*George Phillips
*Manuel Rice
*John S. Ross
Felix Sablan
*Seraphine Silva
Jose Sauza
*W. H. Summers
*Charles Winters
*William H. Young

VOYAGE 20 (DECEMBER 6, 1893–NOVEMBER 5, 1895)

*James A. M. Earle, Master
Frederick D. Swain, 1st Mate (killed at sea by a whale)
*William W. James, 2nd Mate
*George H. Peckham, 3rd Mate
*Joseph Avellar, 4th Mate
James Aao
Vincente Enos Aflague
*Peder Andersen
Inez Avejay
*Carl Baptista
Thomas Barry

Christ Berentsem
Louis Blas
*John Branscombe
*George Brown
Robert Brown
B. Castro
George P. Christian
Gresley Christian
Holder Christian
Parker Christian
Francesco de la Bora
Vincente de Castro
Antone De Costa
*Leonte de Cruz
Antonio de la Cruz
Jose de la Cruz

Juan de la Cruz
Vincente de la Cruz
*Luis Gamatuatan
Francesco Guerra
I. Guerrero
Robert Hampton
William Hanson
*John Jacobs
*W. Kahulio
Joaquim Karado
*Jack Kelley
Harry A. Kluge
*Charles F. Koch
A. LaCoste
Frank Lopes
J. Luhan

Phillip Mann
*Frank Mathews
Henry Meiggs
Jose Mendiolo
Fidel Morris
Jose Nego
Frank A. Perry
John Peters
A. Quinn
Albert Quintell
Hessie Quintell
Walter H. Quintell
Willie Quintell
Juan Rosa
Carl V. Ross
J. Ross

Manuel Ross
T. Ryan
John Sablan (died)
John Santos
Manuel Santos

Mariano Santos
Joe Senner
Joe Siloa
Joe Silva
*John Silvia

Theodore Snell
Charles Spencer
*W. H. Summers
Hugh N. Thyrd
Joseph Vieira

Frank White
William Wolmanes
Albert Zander

VOYAGE 21 (DECEMBER 2, 1895–NOVEMBER 1, 1896)

*James A. M. Earle,
    Master
*George P. Christian, 1st
    Mate
*Antonio Margarido, 2nd
    Mate
*Joe Avellar, 3rd Mate
*Julius B. Perry, 4th Mate
Nicholas Aflague
*Peder Andersen
Carl Baptista
Hugh Henry Bemis
Louis Blas

*George Brown
*Edward Carter
Jose Comacho
*Leonte de Cruz
*Antonio de la Cruz
Rosario de la Rosario
Luis Gamatuatan
*Henry Gomes
Kaynara Gumbargeui
John Hamilton
Thomas Howard
*John Jacobs
Juan Karanio

Kato
Okicirke Kichitoro
*Claud C. King
Kitaosajihi
*Charles F. Koch
Muskaii Kotaro
*Frank Mathews
*Jose Mendiolo
T. Mortimer
*Henry Perreira
*Charles Roeper
*Thomas Ryan
*Charles D. Sanford

Joe Santos
John Santos
Antonio Silva
*Joe Silva
*Chris Starup
Charles Stewart
*Charles Strelow
*W. H. Summers
*Hugh N. Thyrd
Charles Visher
Wakamatsu

VOYAGE 22 (DECEMBER 3, 1896–OCTOBER 25, 1897)

*John S. Layton, Master
*Horace F. Tower, 1st
    Mate
*Antonio Margarido, 2nd
    Mate
*Joe Avellar, 3rd Mate
*Honorio A. Martin, 4th
    Mate
Emanuel Morgan, later
    mate
*Enos Aflague
*Peder Andersen
*A. Andersson
*Carl Baptista
*Joe Basilleo

*George Brown
*Jose Comacho
*Leonte de Cruz
*Antonio de la Cruz
*Jose de los Santos
*Louis Forrester
*Thomas Gomes
*Carl Greton
*Ben Ignacio
Ishitorationo
*John Jacobs
*W. Janman
Sakuminta Junkitan
*Kato
*Jack Kelley

*G. Kitooka
*O. Kitzi
*Charles F Koch
Kemada Kuramruka
*Peter Layron
Leander
Peter Manscrieff
*Frank Mathews
*Jose Mendiolo
Morigo "Jap"
Yokohama Ohasuki
*Henry Olson
*Henry Perreia
*George T. Samuel
Jose Santos

*John Stacy
*Chris Starup
W. H. Summers
*Peter Taitano
Targuerlarmarti
*Hugh N. Thyrd
Chester Tokeka
Frank Webber
*John Williams
Sao Yar
Yokohama
*Charles Young

VOYAGE 23 (NOVEMBER 11, 1897–OCTOBER 28, 1898)

*Thomas Scullun, Master
*Emanuel F. Morgan, 1st
    Mate
*George P. Christian, 2nd
    Mate
*Honorio A. Martin, 3rd
    Mate
*Joseph Thurston, 4th
    Mate
*Enos Aflague
*Peder Andersen
*Joseph Avellar
*J. F. Bartlett
*Carl Baptista
Joe Basilleo

*Fred J. Brown
George Brown
*Torore Bue
Antone Costa
*Cosaki
Cako Crouse
Joaquin de la Cruz
*Jose de los Santos
*John Dooley
*Henry Gomes
*Carl Greton
*Charles F. Koch
*Peter Layton
*James McCormick
Robert F. Marshall

*Joaquin Materne
*Frank Mathews
*Fidel Morris
Nanuilet
K. Ozaki
*Jose Pangelino
*Lino Patricio
Joe Perado
*John Santos
*Jose Santos
George Smith
*W. H. Summers
*Peter Taitano
Takashasha (died)
*Ernest Thompson

Lewis Thurston
*W. Turner
*Koto Walamack
*Frank Webber
*Charley Wills
Osado Yoskisuku

VOYAGE 24 (NOVEMBER 26, 1898–NOVEMBER 2, 1899)

*Thomas Scullun, Master
*Emanuel F. Morgan, 1st Mate
*George P. Christian, 2nd Mate
*Honorio A. Martin, 3rd Mate
*Joseph Thurston, 4th Mate
*Enos Aflague
*Peder Andersen
Joaquin Arriolo
*Joe Avellar
*Mark M. Carroll

*Cosaki
*Joe Cruz
*Joaquin de la Cruz
*Jose de la Cruz
Bread Fruit
*Charles Gilmette
*Henry Gomes
*Carl Greton
Frank Islida
*Charles F. Koch
*Peter Layton
Joe Lesama
*James McCormick
*James McGregor

*Joaquin Materne
*Frank Mathews
*Jose Mendiolo
*Dennis Moran
*Fidel Morris
Antonio Pangalino
*Joe Pangalino
Venison Pangalino
*Lino Patricio
*Juan Peres
Joaquin Polio
*Robert Ritter
*John Rosario
*John Santos

*Jose Santos
*J. Schaffer
*George Smith
*Jose M. Souza
*W. H. Summers
*Thomas W. Swain
*Jose Tagnata
*Peter Taitano
Francisco Tenorio
*Luis Thurston
Sisoko Torria
*Frank Webber
*Osada Yashiske

VOYAGE 25 (DECEMBER 7, 1899–OCTOBER 29, 1900)

*Thomas Scullun, Master
*Emanuel F. Morgan, 1st Mate
*George P. Christian, 2nd Mate
*Honorio A. Martin, 3rd Mate
*Joseph Thurston, 4th Mate
*Peder Andersen
*Joaquin Arriolo
*Jose Augustine
*W. A. Bailey
*Nelson G. Carleton

*Henry Corte
*John de Castro
*Joaquin de la Cruz
Gregorio de la Rama
*Philip Domingo
*John Gareno
*W. L. Hall
W. H. Johnson
*H. Lahmeyer
*Ernest Lemans
John Lewin
*James McCormick
*Joaquin Materne
*Frank Mathews

*Dennis Moran
*Fidel Morris
*Joaquin Palacio
*Antonio Pangalino
*Ben Pangalino
Joe Pangalino
*Frank Patrico
*Lino Patricio
*Juan Peres
Frank Peterson
Ben Petra
Ben Regas
*John Rosario
*Sam Rotama

*Ben Santos
*John Santos
*Jose Santos
*W. E. Sloat
*George P. Smith
*Ernest Sornano
*Thomas Stokes
*Charles Strelow
*W. H. Summers
*Thomas W. Swain
*Joken Tenorio
*C. M. Tower
*Frank Webber
*Ben Whitney

VOYAGE 26 (NOVEMBER 22, 1900–OCTOBER 29, 1901)

*James A. M. Earle, Master
*George F. Allen, 1st Mate
*George P. Christian, 2nd Mate
*Honorio A. Martin, 3rd Mate
*Joseph Thurston, 4th Mate
*Thomas W. Swain, 5th Mate

*Joaquin Arriolo
*Fred Britton
*John Castro
*Christ Christian
*Manuel Claudina
*H. Corte
*Philip Domingo
*Adolphus F. Grose
*Jerry Guam
*Paul Hackentroich
*Otto Hoffman

H. H. Johnson
W. F. Lincoln
*John Lopes
*Manuel Lopes
*James McCormick
*Frank Mathews
*Fidel Morris
*Thomas Oliveira
*Lino Patricio
*John Pereira
*Mike Roderick

*Vicente Sales
*Ben Santos
*John Santos
*Manuel Silvia
*Thomas Stokes
*W. H. Summers
*Rehina Teheda
*C. M. Tower
*John Waller
*Frank Webber
J. A. Welch

VOYAGE 27 (NOVEMBER 27, 1901–OCTOBER 28, 1902)

*Thomas Scullun, Master
*Emanuel F. Morgan, 1st Mate
*Charles D. Sanford, 2nd Mate
*Joseph Thurston, 3rd Mate
*C. M. Tower, 4th Mate

*C. E. Allen
*Peder Andersen
*Antone Bartholdo
*R. W. Black
*George G. Christian
George P. Christian
*Manuel Claudina
*John de Castro

*Fred Ellingsen
*Lonnie Harper
*H. H. Johnson
*John Lewin
*Nelson Lambert
*John Lopes
*Manuel Lopes
*James McCormick

*Jose Mendiolo
*Frank Miller
*H. D. Morton
C. Mullaney
*Thomas Oliveira
*L. B. Palmer
*Ben Pangalino
*Jerry Pangalino

*Jose Pangalino
*John Pereira
*John Peres (died)
*John Peterson

Harry Puiglapp
Isaac Puiglapp
Jack Puiglapp
Tom Puiglapp

*Vicente Sales
*Ben Santos
*Thomas Stokes
*Charles Strelow

*Frank Webber
*Frank Wilson

VOYAGE 28 (NOVEMBER 20, 1902–OCTOBER 27, 1903)

*James A. M. Earle,
  Master
*Emanuel F. Morgan, 1st
  Mate
*George P. Christian, 2nd
  Mate
*Joseph Thurston, 3rd
  Mate
*John Pereira, 4th Mate
*Peder Andersen
*William Barrows
*Antone Bartholdo

*Walter Bechtel
*Manuel Claudina
*Ben Cruz
*Antone M. Eriss
*M. Flaherty
J. Ferkrmeta
*Nicholas Gellers
*Manuel Gonsalves
*Devol Hotchkiss
Kido
*James Kilpatrick
*John Lewin

*Conrad Look
*John Lopes
*Manuel Lopes
Mantero
*James McNeil
*Jose Mendiolo
*H. D. Morton
Yorchiro Okuyama
*Thomas Oliveira
*H. A. Pearey
*John Peterson
*Isaac Puiglapp

*Tom Puiglapp
*Pedro Quantillinia
O. Rabayoski
*Clarence Reynolds
*Charles D. Sanford
*Bartolo Santos
*Manuel Silvia
*Jose M. Souza
*George W. Stratton
W. Kuchi Tachichi
*Leno Tehada
*Frank Webber

VOYAGE 29 (NOVEMBER 18, 1903–OCTOBER 31, 1904)

*James A. M. Earle,
  Master
*Charles A. Sparks, 1st
  Mate
*George P. Christian, 2nd
  Mate
*Joseph Thurston, 3rd
  Mate
*R. L. McLachlan, 4th
  Mate
*Jose M. Souza, 5th Mate
*Peder Andersen
*John Anderson
*H. A. Aurel

*William Barrows
*Arthur Biddle
*R. L. Chambers
*Manuel Claudina
*Jose de Castro
*A. Ekstrom
*Edward Faerber
*Nicholas Gellers
*Manuel Gonsalves
*E. Grundahl
*Eddie Hogan
Asay Jap
Kohara Jap
*B. A. Jones

*Adolf Koch
*Charles Kopatz
*Richard Ludwig
*John Lewin
*Conrad Look
*John Lopes
*James McConnell
*James McNeil
*H. D. Morton
*John Nusal
*Thomas Oliveira
*Jose Penero
*Peter Quintinalla
*James Russell

Motaki Sakichi
*John T. Short
*Manuel Silvia
Sato Spika
*Samuel Stein
*George W. Stratton
*John A. Taylor
Sato Tomachichi
*Frank Webber
Yamda Yakukicha
Kikuchi Yoshimatuski

VOYAGE 30 (NOVEMBER 25, 1904–JUNE 12, 1906)

*Edwin J. Reed, Master
*Emanuel F. Morgan, 1st
  Mate
(No 2nd Mate listed)
*John Pereira, 3rd Mate
*Antone J. Alameda, 4th
  Mate
*Antone Silva, 5th Mate
Jose L. Alameda
Juan Arbares
*William Barrows
*Fred Borneman
*J. B. Brown

*Louis Dablien
*Jesus de la Cruz
Centehan A. Faria
*Charles A. Fisher
Ernest Getten
*Manuel Gonsalves
Norman A. Graves
*Frank Greene
E. Grundahl
Allyne Haynes
*Benjamin A. Jones
*Charles King
Adolph Koch

*Herman Larson
*Richard Ludwig
Terehu Maracaro
*H. D. Morton
*Antone Nicholas
Papa
Tahuroa Peck
*Paul Rasmussen
Juan P. Roderigues
*James Rodgers
*Fred Rodman
*Manuel Rosa
Harry Rose

*Jose Rose
*James Russell
*John Starr
*Samuel Stein
*Harvard Stone
*George W. Stratton
Tuna A. Taunia
Cenaria Tessier
Pahero A. Tuania
Mahuria A. Vehuation
*T. Watson
*Frank Webber

VOYAGE 31 (AUGUST 11, 1906–JULY 4, 1908)

James A. M. Earle, Master,
  resigned
Hiram Nye, Master
  succeeding

Judson James, 1st Mate,
  discharged
George P. Christian, 2nd
  Mate

Frank J. Almeida, 2nd
  Mate succeeding
John Pereira, 3rd Mate

Antone J. Alameda, 4th
  Mate
James Alick
Pedro S. Almeida

Joseph Beetham
Joseph Briggs
Arthur Bowers
William H. T. Broadway
John Brooks
Andrade D. Costa
Joe Cruz
Joao da Rocha
Jose F. da Santos
Antonio G. de Azevada
Victorino de Sousa
Manuel de Rosario

Henry V. Doherty
Honor E. Earle (Master's
    Wife)
Frank English
John Gilbert
Robert T. Goodsall
James Harry
Herbert C. Huchins
Charles Johnson
Wesley Lowe
Terehu Maracaro
John Mars

J. J. Morrissey
H. D. Morton
William T. Neville
Antone Nicholas
Edward Outerbridges
Edward Osborn
John Peck
Francis Pereira
William Peters
Papau Piare
Paul Rasmussen
Joaquin Rosa

Manuel Rosa
Fred Shore
Harry Stein
John Stevens
Edward G. Thayer
Henry Thompson
Walter Thompson
David Wake
Frank Webber
Richard Woods

VOYAGE 32 (SEPTEMBER 2, 1908–SEPTEMBER 12, 1910)

Arthur O. Gibbons, Mas-
    ter, resigned due to
    illness
*Charles S. Church, Mas-
    ter succeeding
Joseph Roderick, 1st
    Mate, discharged
J. J. Senna, 1st Mate,
    found insane,
    discharged
*Joseph Thurston, 2nd
    Mate
*Nicholas Francis, 3rd
    Mate, later 1st Mate
*James Alick

*Thomas H. Bess
*Jose Borja
William H. Brush
H. Carsten
*George P. Christian
*Joe Cruz
Jose da Costa
*Joao da Rocha
*Mathew Deas
*Victorino de Sousa
*Manuel dos Reis
*Henry Doyle
Wilfred N. Francis
*Justa M. Ganetti
*Ramon Garido

William Haggie
Louis Hansen
*James Harry
Robert Holmes
Peter Jackson
*Charles Johnson
*Joseph King
*Alfred Lopes
*John Lopes
*Terehu Maracaro
*Theodore Monteiro
*H. D. Morton
*Antone Nicholas
Benjamin Patricia
*John E. Peck

*Paulo Rames
Paul Rasmussen (died)
*Antonio Rosa
*Enaas Rosa
*Joaquin Rosa
*Manuel Rosario
*Pedro Silva
John Soares
Domingo Sousa
    (stowaway)
*Joseph Thomas
*Frank Webber
*William Wilson

VOYAGE 33 (MAY 10, 1911–AUGUST 9, 1913)

*Charles S. Church,
    Master
*William H. Griffiths, 1st
    Mate
*George P. Christian, 2nd
    Mate
*Thomas Stokes, 3rd
    Mate
*Shadrach D. Tilton, 4th
    Mate
Manuel Almeda
*Peder Andersen
A. P. Avila
*Arthur Barnes
*Clayton H. Bills
*Jose Borja
William Boucher
*James A. Boyd
John Brazil

*Joseph Byrnes
James Caesar
*Charlotte E. Church,
    Master's Wife and Assis-
    tant Navigator
*Manuel Claudino
*Daniel J. Conway
Joe Cruz
M. M. Cruz
*John W. Dawson
*Henry Doyle
*William J. Drohan
*Charles Edwards
Ernest
M. A. Francis
*William Gillam
*Bernard Gomes
J. H. Gomes
*Manuel J. Gomes

*Alvan Goodman
Robert Holmes
Peter Jackson
Isaac L. Joab (died)
Edward Johnson
Harold Johnson
Teddy Kanaka
*Phillip Lelle
Victor D. Lopes
Jose Machado
*Joseph F. McDonald
*Jack J. Merrill
*Herbert Muncey
*John T. O'Brien
Antonio Pangalino
John Peck
*Manuel Pina
Pigarto Prieto
M. J. Reis

*Enaas Rosa
Jose Santos
*Frank Sears
Frederick Scott
*Joseph Shea
Frank Silva
Joe Silvia
M. J. Silvia
M. Soares
Domingo Sousa
*Manuel A. Tegue
Ernst C. Thomas
*Walter J. Tiplow
*Ira Tucker
*Frank Williams
Joseph Wing
Frederick Young

VOYAGE 34 (SEPTEMBER 5, 1916–OCTOBER 23, 1917)

*Benjamin D. Cleveland,
    Master

*John D. Lopes, 1st Mate
*John Leamba, 2nd Mate

*Walter Thompson, 3rd
    Mate

Joe Almeda
Lewis F. Bond

Arthur Bowers
Fred I. Brigham
James E. Clarke
Benjamin W. Cleveland
John Culgin
Antonio Fonseca
Charles Harris
Arthur Jackson

Edward Jon
Aguste Lemas (drowned)
Howard McCormick
Frank McLellan
Frank Matley
Antone Montario
Richard Moore
   (drowned)

Edward W. Morse II
Henry Murphy
Dan O'Connor (drowned)
Frank Payzant
Albert Rubeiro (drowned)
Bert Smith
Sylvester L. Sousa
Joseph Thomas

Earle Wentworth
Edward Winslow
*(Lack of complete records
   prevents full identification
   of those who completed
   voyage 34)*

VOYAGE 35 (JULY 16, 1918–SEPTEMBER 7, 1919)

*Joseph F. Edwards,
   Master
*Theophilo M. Freitas,
   Mate
*Frank Almeda
*John V. Almeida
*Antonio Andreade
*Joao J. Aniseto

*Jacinto Costa
*Harry Cruse
*Joao B. Duarte
*Manuel Flora
*Benjamin Freitas
*Pedro Freitas
*Antonio R. Gomes

*William W
   Higginbotham
*Manuel D. Jackson
*William Knowles Jr.
*Jose F. Lopes
*Nahum Nickelson II
*Manuel Oliveira
*Manuel Ramos

*Antonio J. Rosa
*Joe Santos
*Jose A. Soares
*Joseph Stephenson
*Paul Tarvas
*Harold E. Tilton

VOYAGE 36 (OCTOBER 18, 1919–JULY 16, 1920)

*Joseph F. Edwards,
   Master
*Peter B. Alves, 1st Mate
*Benjamin Freitas, 2nd
   Mate
*Thomas Lima, 3rd Mate

*Frank W. Almeda
*John J. Amigo
*Henry Correa
*Bartholome J. Encainede
*Antonio M. Freitas
*Pedro A. Freitas

*Manuel Gomes
*Miguel Lopes
*Silveiro Lopes
*Joao P. Monteiro
*Dennis Pena
*Joao Ramos

*Manuel J. Rosario
*Luis M. Silva
*Vincente Silva
*Nicolau Talantino
*Jules Tavares

VOYAGE 37 (SEPTEMBER 9, 1920–MAY 28, 1921)

*John Gonsalves, Master
*Frank M. Freitas, 1st
   Mate
*Antonio Tavares, 2nd
   Mate
*Frank Spencer, 3rd Mate

*Antonio D. Soares, 4th
   Mate
*Jose Barros
*Joe Cruize
*Nicolas A. Cruze
*Manuel J. Fonseca
*Antonio Gomes

*Antonio M. Lopes
*Eugenio P. Lopes
*M. Lopes
*Antonio S. Monteiro
*Dennis Pena
*Edward Ramos
*John A. Reis

*Manuel Rosario
*Louis Santos
*Micke Silva
*Mario R. Soares
*Pedro S. Soares
*Valentine Soares
*Jose Tavare

Index

Numbers in *bold italics* indicate illustrations